ANATOMY

OF

PROJECT

MANAGEMENT

Jim Mackay

Createspace conversion and cover design
by Araby Greene, epubble.com

Cover illustrations:
Arrows © puckillustrations – Fotolia.com
Mannequin © selensergen – Depositphotos.com

Contents

Preface

Projects have been integral to the success of the human race for many thousands of years. The legacy of ancient civilisations – the pyramids of Egypt, the city of Rome, the Aztec Temples – are all testament to our historical achievements in the management of challenging projects. Projects are the lifeblood that sustains our continued advancement and our dominance over the environment we inhabit.

Everything we see around us in the modern world – the towns and the cities, the highways and the vehicles we drive, the vast railway networks, the airports and the aeroplanes – have all been created as a result of our ability to manage challenging projects. Gas, electricity and clean water are delivered direct to our homes because of our capacity to work together to achieve project success. In relatively recent times projects have enabled us to travel through space, to walk on the moon, and to explore the outermost reaches of our universe. Our technical expertise, allied with our project management ability, has resulted in worldwide communication networks and the technical wizardry that we take for granted daily – and these latest project successes are now pivotal in fuelling our continued advancement into the future.

We are good at projects – we might even conclude that projects are in our genes. But the world is becoming increasingly complex, and achieving beneficial change through projects is becoming progressively more challenging as a result. Despite the many successes there are still high profile project failures, and the proportion of projects that meet all of their objectives, and that also complete on time and on budget, is not very high. There are many good reasons why this should be the case and some of these reasons are highlighted in the chapters that follow.

The intention of this book is not to analyse the reasons for project "failure" or to provide a detailed recipe for "success" – there are just too many variables in project management to attempt this. But all senior managers, all project managers, and all aspiring project managers should at least understand the fundamentals of project management – the basic principles that apply to all projects. Through this understanding they will be able to avoid the most obvious pitfalls when embarking upon significant change through projects.

A project becomes increasingly complex and demanding as it progresses through its life cycle and it is essential to maintain a high level perspective throughout. For this reason I have deliberately focussed on the main disciplines of project management – the vital organs that must function correctly if the project is to achieve its goal. I have kept all the illustrations and examples simple – there are plenty of books and training courses available that delve into the minutiae of project techniques and tools, and there is no need to add to these here.

In this small book I have tried to distil all the common sense that I have accumulated over the course of a long project management career. In addition to outlining the fundamental project management disciplines, I have emphasised the practical difficulties that are faced by all project managers. The theory and the practice of project management are rarely in harmony. This does not mean that the theory is inadequate – in fact it is well established – but application of the theory requires considerable flexibility and an emphasis on inter-personal skills. I have sought to highlight this aspect of project management by describing some real life scenarios that I have encountered during my career.

My own views have been reinforced by the knowledge gained during my time assessing senior project managers for certification qualifications – a responsibility that included detailed scrutiny of hundreds of complex projects across a wide variety of industries. I have always been struck by the similarity of the problems encountered by all project managers everywhere, and how closely these problems resonate with the challenges that I faced myself. My intention in this book is to represent my own experiences and the experiences of the many project managers that I have met during the course of my career.

1: Management of Change

Cynicism or realism?

"There is nothing more difficult to plan, more doubtful of success, nor more dangerous to manage than the creation of a new system.

For the initiator has the enmity of all who would profit from the preservation of the old system, and merely lukewarm defenders in those who would gain from the new one"

—Niccolo Macciavelli, 1513

We may be more familiar with, and receptive to, change in the modern world than were our ancestors in the 16th century, but there is still a loud ring of truth in the statement above. In my own experience of managing projects Machiavelli is being realistic – he had the ability to see beneath the facade of human posturing, and to expose the truth relating to many aspects of human endeavour.

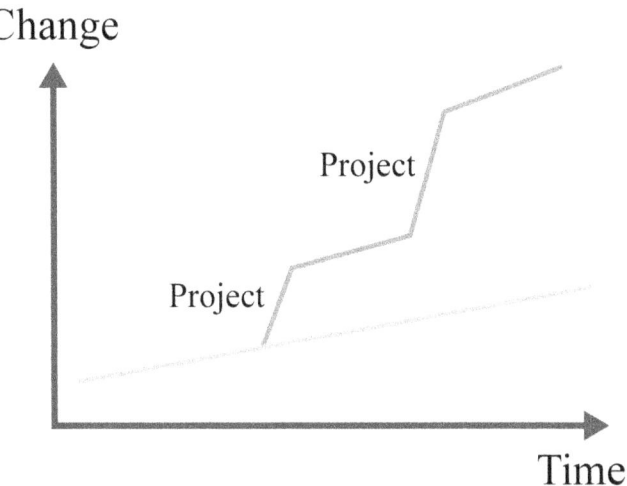

Change is of course a constant feature in our lives. Nature relentlessly changes our world, be it the gradual transition from one season to the next over the course of a year, or the very slow evolution of life forms on our planet over millions of years. And of course we change within ourselves every day as we age. Now the human factor has been introduced into worldly affairs, and humans have decided to change this world more rapidly. In order to achieve this we have invented projects.

Projects are inherent in our human desire to develop and improve – they are a part of our genetic heritage. But therein lies a contradiction. We have a strong desire to change and improve the world, but we must overcome the anxiety that this creates in those affected by the projects that engineer change – projects will always experience resistance from some quarters. This is the backdrop to project management in most situations; it needs to be recognised and the consequences managed from start to finish of a project.

A project must be considered worthwhile by most, if not all, of those most affected by its consequences – the stakeholders. Their support needs to be in evidence initially in order for the project to get off the ground, and it needs to continue throughout the project's duration to help overcome the challenges to progress that will almost certainly emerge. If this support is no more than lukewarm then the project is likely to falter at the first signs of significant difficulty.

Given the certainty of challenge, and the potential for failure, there is a great sense of achievement when a project is successful – especially for the project manager. To have taken on the responsibility for managing a significant project, and to have delivered the expected benefits, provides personal satisfaction and undoubtedly enhances career prospects.

In our general experience of life, if we get most things right most of the time we will most likely be successful; in project management we must get everything right, all of the time. Getting everything right is of course unrealistic. When we plan a significant project we are attempting to forecast a very complex future, and as reality unfolds it will inevitably differ from our plans. And we cannot just consider our project in isolation – as we focus on our own undertaking the rest of the world is also busy making changes, some of which may impact on our plans and even render them untenable. This is particularly the case for very large projects with protracted timescales.

> A prominent indicator of the problems associated with rapid change is the frequency with which the Public Accounts Committee in the UK investigates major project failings. On one occasion I had the interesting experience of meeting with some members of this committee:
>
> *The closest I have ever been to the seat of power in the UK was during a lunch in the Houses of Parliament, Westminster. Our directors had arranged the lunch for some members of the*

two main political parties, including members of the highly influential Public Accounts Committee, at our company's expense. The idea was that I would give a short presentation on Project Management issues between the starter and the main course, and then we would all have a discussion on the issues raised. Matters did not quite unfold according to the script.

Half of the members of parliament (MPs) we had invited turned up late, and I ended up giving my talk while the main course was being served and eaten. In itself not a major disaster, but the discussion that followed certainly was. One MP would start talking and carry on talking, hogging the discussion until another MP managed to interrupt successfully. Then this MP would carry on talking, and talking, until someone else managed to muscle in. There is obviously a certain knack in getting the floor, but I never mastered it.

The MPs from opposing parties ended up trying to score points off each other, and never properly addressed the important issues that had been raised. I learned an important lesson during my project management career – listen! I don't have the attributes necessary to become an MP, and I suspect that most MPs would not survive long in my world of project management. My lunch companions were very polite to me at the end of the event, but I did feel somewhat deflated. And I had changed my mind about one thing – there is such a thing as a free lunch!

Project management is concerned with the management of change, usually very rapid change, and this creates uncertainty and risk. But imagine a life full of certainty and devoid of risk – it does not sound very interesting, and it certainly does not reflect our natural progression over the course of our evolutionary journey. Projects are exciting and challenging, and they are often extremely complex. In order to give ourselves the best chance of success we must begin by understanding the following fundamental principles:

The Triple Constraint – every project that is undertaken in the business world is subject to this characteristic. The aim of every project is to deliver a defined scope of work, within a set period of time, and for a considered cost.

The Project Goal – the objective of the project, the project's ultimate goal, needs to be clearly stated and understood by all those directly involved with or impacted by it. The critical attributes associated with this project goal must also be clearly understood.

Organisation – the project organisation needs to embrace all the stakeholders, contractors, sub-contractors and suppliers, as well as the core project team. Processes need to be established that ensure communication and cohesion right across this organisation.

Planning – plans must be realistic; the scope of the project together with the anticipated timescales and costs should provide a balanced representation of what is achievable. For large and complex projects this is understandably challenging.

Estimating – what work needs to be done and how much effort does this work require? Estimating is at the heart of planning and integral to the planning exercise. Elegant and elaborate plans are of little use if estimating has not been carried out with diligence.

Risks – projects attract many risks; the most potentially damaging of these risks need to be proactively managed before they mature and threaten the success of the project.

Quality – quality is not an add-on to projects; quality should be built into the fabric of project plans, and integral to all activities throughout the entire project life cycle.

Teamwork – effective teamwork is essential if success is to be achieved; projects stand or fall on the ability and the desire of those involved to co-operate with each other.

Controlling the project – when a project has gained momentum it uses up resources, especially money, at a rapid rate. Ensuring that processes are effective, maintaining control over the work in progress, dealing urgently with issues, managing risks, and looking ahead to potential problems further down the line, are all of vital importance.

End Game – whatever is being delivered by the project will eventually become part of the wider world. Preparations for the culmination of the project, and the transition of the deliverables into an operational environment, need to be considered and planned well in advance. The end game will most probably require a great deal of effort, over and above normal work patterns, by all of those involved with the project.

In the remainder of this book I will expand on these fundamental principles to provide an insight into how they influence project success. Some aspects of project management are specific to the nature of individual projects and will determine or influence the way in which these principles are applied in practice. I have included overviews of these aspects in the Appendices.

Appendix I: Bid to Project – the commercial context of the project

Appendix II: Project Life Cycles – adoption of an appropriate life cycle

Appendix III: Methodologies – processes mandated by the company or companies involved

There are many techniques and tools available to assist with the management of projects, and some of these are mentioned in passing in the chapters that follow. Detailed information on how these can be applied in a project environment is readily obtainable with a little research. I have included an example of the application of Earned Value Management in Appendix IV. This technique is particularly useful in measuring a project's progress in the context of the triple constraint's scope, time and cost parameters, and illustrating this progress in a meaningful way.

Project managers need to understand how these techniques and tools can benefit their project, but they should not be relied upon to deliver success, or to become an end in themselves. Techniques and tools should never be confused with management. Project success will depend above all on sound management practices, and especially on behavioural skills such as leadership, motivation, and the ability to resolve conflicts and crises.

2: Triple Constraint

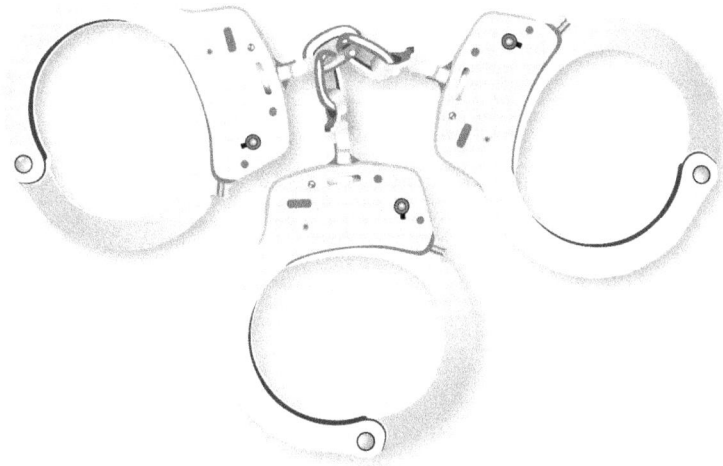

The definition of a project given below incorporates the features (highlighted) that distinguish projects from "business as usual".

A project is an endeavour in which human, material and financial resources are:

*organised in a **novel** way …*

*to undertake a **unique scope** of work …*

*within **constraints of cost and time** …*

*in order to achieve **beneficial change** …*

defined by quantitative and qualitative objectives

Projects require a variety of resources, the most significant of which are people and money. For each project, people are organised in a *novel* way – an organisation is created that has not existed before. Many of the participants will never have worked together prior to the project, and many will be meeting each other for the very first time. Nonetheless, in order to carry out the work efficiently, they need to gel quickly into an effective team to undertake the project. Some may be used to project work, for example in IT systems development projects or major construction works, while for others the experience of working in project teams to achieve rapid change will be new.

The scope of the work to be carried out will be *unique*; it will never have been done before. Many similar projects may have been carried out in the past, but not with exactly the same scope, and not with exactly the same group of people. All commercial undertakings are subject to constraints of cost and time, but it is this uniqueness that is the main differentiator between projects and business as usual – the work carried out in the branch office of a bank, or on a manufacturing production line, follows well established processes on a daily basis.

Every project is subject to *constraints of cost and time*. No-one is going to write a blank cheque in order to achieve the objectives of a project, and no-one is going to wait forever to reap the benefits of their financial investment. Whenever projects are discussed – whether by senior management, by project managers, or by the media – the costs and timescales are inevitably the prominent topics of conversion. Most project work is underpinned by legal contracts in order to safeguard the commercial interests of the parties concerned. These contracts invariably quantify timescales and costs, while the scope is most likely to be represented by a document of some description – for example a requirements specification.

Projects are undertaken to achieve ***beneficial change***, to achieve a new order that has advantages over the old order of things – perhaps a new stretch of road, or a more efficient computer system. The results of the project must be seen to be an improvement and not just a replacement of like for like – and they must represent value for the investment made.

All commercial projects are subject to the triple constraint, which can be depicted by a triangle.

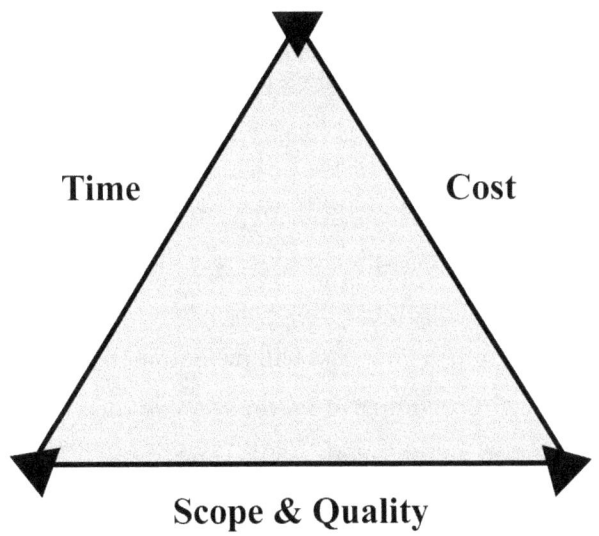

Beneficial change is symbolised by the ***scope and quality*** dimension of the triple constraint, the base line of the triangle. This base line also represents all of the work that has to be done in order to achieve the beneficial change as required by the project goal.

Similar depictions show only scope on the base line, and show quality in the centre of the triangle. But in my experience quality is best incorporated into the scope of the project since it requires work to be done. This work will be necessary to ensure that the fundamental quality requirements are met – that the product is fit for purpose. If a high quality (luxury) product is to be created, more work will be necessary to include advanced features or accessories of some description.

The triple constraint image is a simple but effective depiction of a project. A triangle is an extremely stable construct and cannot be pulled out of shape without affecting the lengths of the sides. If one side is increased in length it will cause an increase to one or both of the other sides, resulting in yet another stable construct.

This is equally true for a project. If the line representing the scope and quality is increased in length, then the lines representing the costs and/or timescales will also increase in length. It may be possible to retain the original timescale when the scope increases, but the line representing the cost will have to increase. There is no other way to retain the integrity of the triangle. It is geometrically possible to increase the scope and time dimensions without increasing the cost, but this is a highly unlikely scenario in the business world. It is also geometrically possible to increase the scope and cost dimensions without increasing the time – but there is a limit to how much work can be achieved in a fixed time, irrespective of how much money is made available.

Of course mathematics does not reflect real life particularly well. Trade-offs between scope and cost, and scope and timescales may be possible, as will trade-offs in terms of quality. But if scope and quality are compromised then it is highly likely that the original objectives of the project goal will also be compromised.

In the real world we cannot predict each twist and turn that may arise during the course of a project. For example, the timely availability of resources to carry out the work according to the schedule is never entirely within the project manager's control. This causes significant problems on most projects, problems that relate directly to the time dimension of the triple constraint. The cost of the various resources required may also vary from those anticipated when the project was initially planned, and impact the cost dimension. These and other factors will cause stresses within the triple constraint that was conceived initially, and will upset the balance.

In the real world we cannot know at the outset all the things that make up the project scope, and therefore the work that needs to be done. The gradual emergence of detail as the project unfolds quite often results in *scope creep*, and this can impact all three dimensions of the triple constraint. Scope creep usually arises because some elements of the scope have been overlooked, or are more complex than originally anticipated, or because the recipient of the project deliverable has had a change of mind. It is rare to experience scope creep in reverse i.e. a reduction in scope, unless it is decided to jettison some of the project objectives in order to meet a critical delivery date. The implications of scope creep, and the mechanisms to help control it, are discussed in Chapter 10: Controlling the Project.

It is essential to allow for some flexibility in all three dimensions of the triple constraint when a project is initially conceived and expectations are set. We cannot forecast the complex future that a project will encounter with mathematical certainty, and it would be imprudent to set expectations too early. Initial attempts to shape the triple constraint are usually based on insufficient information and result in very poor predictions. This is the worst case that I have come across:

I worked as a consultant project manager for a leading finance house that was planning to replace its legacy accounting systems. These systems had been the backbone of its IT for many years. Because of their familiarity with the existing systems, the IT management assumed that a replacement would be quite straightforward – after all the scope was already defined to a large extent by the old system and its supporting processes.

The initial estimate of cost was in the region of £250,000, with a timetable of about one year to develop – but this was mooted before any serious work had been carried out. By the time the new system was fully developed and implemented the cost was in excess of £5 million, and the project had taken over 4 years to complete.

There are two lessons here – replacing legacy systems that have been deeply embedded in the business for a long time is very challenging, and attempting to predict costs and timescales based on familiarity with these legacy systems is fraught with danger. Thorough investigation, analysis and planning are necessary before the triple constraint can be formulated with any confidence.

There are more comprehensive models that can be used to represent projects, but the triple constraint illustrates very effectively the primary forces at work, and allows no latitude for obfuscation. If a project is to be successful it has to be in the right ballpark in terms of scope, timescales and costs from the outset. If these are unrealistic, if they do not form a balanced whole, the project will soon run into difficulties; this will cause concern, possibly panic and anger, among the stakeholder community. Balancing out the triple constraint is the biggest challenge facing planners during the formative stage of a project, and the project manager may not have influence in setting these crucial parameters. See Appendix I: Bid to Project.

As mentioned earlier in this chapter, most project work is carried out under the terms of a contract of some description. Many contracts effectively define the triple constraint and this can give rise to problems for the project manager. The contract price may be stated as say £1.5 million, and the delivery date fixed at 30th September, possibly with financial penalties for late delivery. But the scope and quality cannot be quantified and subsequently measured in the same straightforward terms – they are expressed in words and diagrams that are open to interpretation by the various parties to the contract.

It is important that contracts are sensible, fair to all the parties involved, and reflect any major uncertainties that surround the proposed project. This is not always the case:

Our company had developed a complex software product for the insurance industry and had successfully sold it to several clients. Unfortunately each client required their own specific features that resulted in tailoring of the product. This resulted in several versions of the application software, and each version required additional support and maintenance work. One client in particular had negotiated his own, non-standard, version of the contract and he was particularly inflexible. As a business proposition it was completely unworkable and the management team responsible was shown the door.

While a new management team was being recruited I visited each client in order to understand the difficulties they were experiencing, and to act as a bridge across the management gap. The client who had negotiated a separate contract was in fact a director and part owner of the company, and had a reputation as a tough negotiator. A short while into our meeting he pulled his copy of the contract out of the drawer and slapped it on the table. He said words to the effect – I stitched up your company with this contract and it is now going to cost you a lot of money. He went on to boast that contract negotiation was a game for him, and his main objective was always to secure a contract that was heavily biased in his company's favour.

The main problem from a project management perspective was that the scope of the work to be carried out by our company was not defined in sufficient detail within the contract, and there were substantial penalties for us if we failed to meet all the contractual terms. This story did not have a particularly happy ending for our company in financial terms.

The director in question was very clever and powerful, but had questionable business ethics. In this particular case, those responsible for contract negotiations had forgotten our company mantra:

Fixed Price for Fixed Work

Failing to meet contractual requirements is of course quite common in business, and it is normal practice for a company to attempt to gain advantage in contractual terms. But a heavily biased contract is bad news for the project manager, who quite often has no influence over its terms and conditions. These will most probably have been determined during the bid process, and contracts already signed and exchanged, before the project manager takes responsibility for delivery.

A project and its associated contracts should be based upon a triple constraint that is as realistic as our powers of prediction can achieve. Harmonisation of the key dimensions – scope, time and cost – will lay the foundations for effective control when the project is in progress; but failure to achieve this harmonisation will cause major problems sooner or later. Rectification of a major imbalance when the project is at an advanced stage will incur significant costs, not just in terms of the project, but also in terms of lost business opportunity associated with late delivery.

3: Project Goal

...it's all about winning

The starting point for every project is the definition of the project goal – the objective that must be achieved if it is to be considered a success in terms of beneficial change.

In football the goal is self-evident, as is success in a particular game – score more goals than the opposition. In project terms it is never as simple as that. The project goal requires careful consideration and analysis before assembling a team, and embarking on what will be a long, uncertain and expensive journey. It is essential that we fully understand what we are aiming to achieve, and we need to know exactly where the goal is, otherwise we are unlikely to score one.

It is all about winning – about overcoming the challenges that come from opposition to the changes generated by the project.

This opposition can materialise in many different forms, for example reluctant stakeholders, lack of resources, apathy, unfamiliar technology, issues and risks, bad weather and external influences in the form of changing regulations or legislation. From start to finish there will be hurdles placed in front of the project team. It is helpful to view the management of a project as a competition – to overcome the opposition and achieve the project goal.

Defining the Goal:

A simple statement of the project goal, similar to a mission statement, is a good starting point …

"I believe that this nation should commit itself to achieving the goal, before this decade is out, of landing a man on the moon and returning him safely to the earth."

… and so began one of the greatest adventures of discovery in the history of the human race. These words were spoken by President John F Kennedy in 1961 and culminated in man's first steps on the moon in July 1969.

The force of this statement cannot be underestimated – it incorporates the commitment of the most powerful nation on earth, the promise of an unprecedented voyage through space, the first presence of a human being on another celestial body and a demanding timescale. These are all what we can describe as the *critical attributes* of the project goal. The most critical of all attributes of course is that relating to the return of the astronaut safely to earth. A project to place a man atop a massive rocket and fire it on a trajectory to land on the moon, could no doubt have been realised for a mere fraction of the cost that was involved in returning him safely to Earth.

The imperative when describing any project goal is to state the objective in straightforward terms, and then to identify the critical attributes of that goal.

> ➢ Build a road bridge over the river Forth at Kincardine
> ➢ Improve the efficiency of the Claims Department

The above are examples of projects goals, but there is no indication of the critical attributes associated with these goals. There is insufficient information to determine whether the project will be a success upon completion or not, because there is nothing to *measure.*

> ➢ Build a road bridge over the river Forth at Kincardine that is capable of carrying a maximum of 100 vehicles in one minute, with a maximum single vehicle load of 50 tons
> ➢ Improve the efficiency of the Claims Department to enable a reduction of staffing levels by 10%

These are still very straightforward statements of project goals, but we have now begun to introduce the critical attributes, the level of information that makes measurement of success possible. It is not difficult to conceive of further measurable attributes in these two hypothetical examples.

> ➢ Capacity to accommodate vehicles up to 25 feet in width
> ➢ Work station footprint to exceed the minimum standard by 20% for all staff

In addition to enabling a measurement of success, quantification is important in directing and controlling the efforts of a project team – it needs something tangible to aim for. It is only through quantification that we can clarify the goal and establish the critical attributes that can be measured and controlled.

You can't control what you can't measure

Quantitative measures may not be the only features of the project goal – there may also be qualitative attributes to be considered.

> ➢ The design of the bridge should blend in with the local landscape
> ➢ Improve job satisfaction by providing a wider variety of roles for everyone than at present

It is fairly obvious that a project goal, and its associated critical attributes, should be developed and refined in this way – and this is generally what seems to happen. However, in large organisations when major projects (and especially business change projects) are undertaken, the opportunities for misunderstandings are many. In addition there is the added complication of resistance to change, and the influence of individuals with personal agendas that don't quite coincide with the intended objectives of the project goal.

You may be thinking that the subject matter of this chapter is somewhat simplistic, and that no one is going to make a serious mistake in defining the project goal and its critical attributes. Here is a sombre tale:

A major computer services company ran a payroll service for over a thousand clients and had responsibility for paying millions of their employees each month. Over the years the company had acquired half a dozen different payroll systems, running on a variety of computer platforms. They decided to develop a brand new system to run on the latest mainframe computer, and then convert all the existing payrolls onto this one system.

Having spent over a million pounds on the new system development, it became obvious that there were severe performance issues – the system might not be capable of processing the millions of payrolls in the narrow production window at each month end. I was asked to take a look at the problem. Following some performance tests and advice from technical experts, it was obvious that the architecture of the system was unsuitable for the payroll application, and no amount of affordable computer power and tuning would resolve the problem.

When deciding to develop the new system, one of the most critical of attributes had been overlooked, or had not been taken account of properly during the design phase. Payroll is not a particularly glamorous business function, but it soon goes to the top of the agenda if it fails to pay salaries on time. The performance of the system was critical and there was no option except to redevelop the entire application all over again.

My reward for getting to the bottom of this problem was to be given the task of managing the development of the replacement system. This time an appropriate architecture was designed and all the old payroll systems were converted successfully to the new system. All the clients were provided with a modern front end system in their own payroll offices and there was plenty of capacity for future business expansion. But it had cost the company a great deal more than it should have, and it had lost opportunities for new business while the redevelopment was carried out.

Developing the Goal:

When developing the project goal it is essential to discuss the objectives and critical attributes in depth with all the right people – those who can influence the change, those who will pay for it, and those who will be impacted by it. However much opinion and information emerges from the initial round of discussions and analysis, it is important to achieve a clear understanding of, and agreement on, the beneficial changes that the project will deliver. Too much information could result in a muddying of the waters, misunderstandings, and consequential dissent. Ideally the statement of a project goal, its primary aims and its critical attributes, should be represented on a few pages. Technical details can be included in supplementary documents as appropriate. Clarity is of fundamental importance during the formative stage of every project.

If you are not clear what it is you want …
… you should not be surprised when you don't get it.

When agreement has been reached on the project goal and its critical attributes, the next step is to undertake the first phase of the project life cycle – the concept or feasibility phase. This phase is aimed at establishing what would be involved in undertaking the project, and the business implications associated with it. The main deliverable from this initial phase is a reasoned business case which justifies proceeding further, or alternatively consigns the idea to the filing cabinet. Everything that is proposed at this early stage should be carefully weighed up against other business priorities and discussed between the management who will be most involved and impacted.

When considering the business implications of undertaking a project during the concept or feasibility phase, it is essential to take into account the situation as it exists now, the situation that is anticipated at the end of the project, and how the transition to this new situation will be accomplished. Transition is discussed in Chapter 11: End Game. The disruption to the business over the course of the project must also be considered. All of these aspects need to be examined before a decision to proceed with the project can be taken.

Deliberation of the project goal, its critical attributes and the business implications will help in deciding the most appropriate life cycle for the project. There are several commonly used industry specific life cycles, but each project is unique and a suitable life cycle should be developed to account for all the circumstances associated with the proposed undertaking. Appendix II: Life cycles, illustrates a generic phased cycle; the principles outlined in the following chapters apply, whichever life cycle is adopted.

Everything that is stated above is fairly obvious and straightforward – no more than good business practice. And it needs to be good, because this is the foundation on which a major change initiative, involving considerable cost, complexity and risk, will rest. Strong foundations need to be laid down during the concept or feasibility phase of the project – ambiguity and obfuscation will almost certainly lead to disaster. If we can't get this bit right – a few words on a few pages – what chance does the project that follows have of achieving success?

In the words of Robert Burns in his poem "To a Mouse":

> *The best laid schemes o' Mice an' Men,*
> *Gang aft agley,*
> *An' lea'e us nought but grief an' pain,*
> *For promis'd joy!*

4: Organisation

When the project goal has been clearly defined and the critical attributes identified, the next step is to create a model of the project organisation. This may or may not have been drafted as part of the feasibility study or concept phase, but either way it should be confirmed before detailed plans are produced and the following phase of the project has been started. The project manager may already have been involved in drafting an organisation and in setting expectations, but quite often the project manager is assigned after preliminary work has been carried out. See Appendix I: Bid to Project.

Either way, this is the point at which he or she must get in the driving seat, finalise the organisation, and decide how it will function. The project manager needs to establish him or herself at centre stage from now on until the project is complete. It is the position and influence of the project manager that will determine the effectiveness of the organisation, irrespective of seniority in relation to other stakeholders.

It is the project manager alone who will understand how the organisation is intended to function in detail, and it is the project manager who will accrue detailed knowledge of all aspects of the project as it unfolds. He or she must be given the responsibility and authority that is necessary to make the day-to-day decisions on the project – otherwise it will not be properly managed. Projects cannot be managed efficiently by committee.

A pictorial representation is the most effective way of communicating the project organisation:

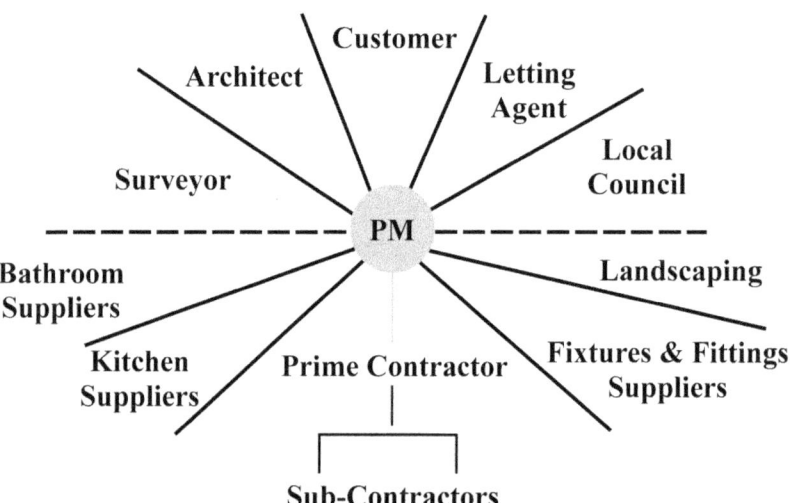

The chart illustrates the project management of the conversion and refurbishment of a large old mansion into a number of flats. The project manager is acting on behalf of a property developer – the customer.

The customer and the project manager are both involved initially when the configuration and the design of the flats are agreed. They work with the architect to create the specifications for the refurbished property, and apply to the local council for planning permission. A prime contractor is given the contract for the main building works, including trade skills such as electricians and plumbers which may be subcontracted. The project manager retains responsibility for supply of the kitchens and bathrooms, other fixtures and fittings, and also for landscaping of the grounds. In this scenario the dotted line represents a distinction between the aspects of the project/organisation for which the project manager has sole responsibility (below the line), and those for which he and the customer have joint responsibility (above the line).

It is the concept of this organisation that is important, not the details. The project manager is the focal point of an organisation that embraces all of the stakeholders. This representation highlights the central role that the project manager undertakes, and it emphasises the communication aspect of this role which is essential for the organisation to function effectively.

Stakeholders:

Without an effective organisation, a project team will not perform efficiently, and it is important to set this up correctly before finalising detailed plans. Every stakeholder in the organisation will have influence over the project and will generate dependencies between the activities to be carried out. These dependencies must therefore be reflected in the plans.

Stakeholders are often viewed as somehow outside the day-to-day running of the project team. In reality, their contribution is every bit as important as that of the people in the core team whose job it is to create the product. In the example above the core team consists of the prime contractor and various sub-contractors. It is important to consider everyone in the organisation as a stakeholder – from the people knocking down walls to the local council. They all have influence upon the project and generate dependencies between activities; projects require team effort and everyone has a contribution to make.

To join a game of poker a player must put in a stake, and will hope to reap some benefit from this stake. The same is true of projects – a stakeholder must be prepared to make an appropriate contribution in order to reap the rewards of a successful project. Stake holding is always a two-way street:

> ➢ Every member of the team is required to carry out specific activities or tasks conscientiously, and in return he or she will want job satisfaction and a positive update to their CV
> ➢ The customer wants the project team to create a quality product, and in return the project requires the

customer to clarify the requirements and accept the product

➢ Sub-contractors require clear specifications for the work that they carry out, and in return the project expects timely delivery of the components they are creating

➢ The project manager's boss expects him or her to deliver on time and to budget, and in return the project manager requires their support in providing the necessary resources and resolving certain issues

The organisation for even a small or moderately sized project can become quite complex when all stakeholders are included – and it is easy to overlook one or two. This can have serious consequences:

I was leading a team developing a new computer system for the management of over 1 million insurance policies. The work was progressing well and, after nearly a year, the end users of the system were happy with the test results and looking forward to the introduction of the system into their live operations.

At a very late stage the trade unions intervened and demanded to hold discussions on the implications of the new system. But there were two separate trade unions involved and they refused to sit down together with the project team to address their concerns.

In the end we had separate meetings with representatives from each of the trade unions and produced a combined list of the issues that they had raised. Fortunately the system was well founded and the users were enthusiastic – there were only a few fairly minor issues to resolve and both trade unions were agreed on these.

But it could quite easily have ended in a stand-off, where nobody wins. The lessons here are clear – think long and hard about who the stakeholders are at the beginning of a project, and don't forget the trade unions!

It is the project manager's responsibility to ensure that everyone associated with the project understands their role in the project organisation, and how this role relates to the project objective. When there are several stakeholders in management or senior management positions it is advisable to appoint a project sponsor – someone at a senior level who can represent the project manager's concerns and exert influence on other stakeholders who may be hindering project progress.

Complex Projects:

Projects are becoming progressively more complex, and a single project may involve several industry disciplines such as IT (hardware & software), manufacturing and construction. The work to be carried out may be spread across geographically dispersed sites. Large projects are commonly split into several sub-projects, each with its own team leader or project manager, and these sub-projects may be located in different areas of the country, or even in different countries. Under these circumstances the level of complexity may be too much for an individual to manage, and it is not uncommon to find a project management team at the head of affairs. This team may comprise a project director and one or more project managers. If large parts of the work have been sub-contracted to other businesses then these businesses will also have appointed their own project managers.

Very large projects, for example joint ventures where several major businesses are involved, require an overall representation of the project organisation that clearly defines the lines of communication between businesses. They will also require a number of other organisational schemas for each of the main participating businesses. For all project organisations, large or small, complex or straightforward, there must to be a well-defined division of responsibilities; each project manager involved should have a clear understanding of his or her own area of responsibility, and how this relates to other project managers in the wider context of the project.

Roles & Responsibilities:

A clear pictorial representation of the project organisation is a good starting point when identifying the individual or individuals within each sector of the organisation who have responsibilities in relation to a project. For each individual a description of his or her role on the project, and how it relates to individuals in other sectors, can be drawn up. Each named person should agree his or her role and sign up to it. It is the responsibility of the project manager to make sure that this happens – he or she is the only person who understands in depth how all the various contributions fit together across the project organisation, and the crucial dependencies between these contributions.

Project Boards, Steering Groups, Progress Meetings, Team Meetings:

The plans, and the progress against these plans, need to be communicated to everyone involved in the project. The nature and frequency of meetings, as well as the participants required to attend, will depend upon the size of the project and the structure of its organisation. It is good practice to schedule all the regular meetings at the start of the project to ensure that they are incorporated into everyone's diaries well in advance. See also Chapter 10: Controlling the Project.

Change Meetings & Risk Management Meetings:

In small to medium-sized projects, change and risk discussions may be incorporated within the meetings listed above, but on larger projects it may be more effective to discuss these aspects in separate meetings. Individual change meetings are essential on large and/or complex projects, as each proposed change must be carefully analysed by those who understand its implications. The decisions taken on incorporating changes to the original scope of the project can have far-reaching effects on the project's success, as discussed in Chapter 10: Controlling the Project.

Progress Reporting:

Regular progress reports – weekly, fortnightly or monthly – will be prepared during the course of the project. The frequency, content and recipients for each level of report should be agreed at the start of the project. In a small to medium-sized project, one progress report may suffice; on larger projects with two or even more levels of decision making, separate reports will probably be necessary. For example a detailed progress report may be provided for management discussion and decision making, and a summary report prepared for executives.

Everyone in the organisation needs to be made aware of the information that they have to provide on a regular basis to enable the progress report to be prepared. The project manager will then produce a consolidated progress report which encompasses all activities and issues across the wider project organisation.

Project File:

Projects generate vast quantities of information, for example contracts, specifications, estimates, plans, progress reports, minutes of meetings, costing and emails. A structured filing system should be put in place to allow easy access to this information. At some stage the project will probably be audited and the project file will be the auditor's first port of call.

Physical Environment:

Ideally everyone involved in the project would be located in the same or adjacent space. This is probably unrealistic in many situations, but the number of different locations should be kept to a minimum. Proximity of project team members promotes better communication and cooperation. Emails are useful for following up on face-to-face meetings, or telephone conversations, but should not be relied upon as the primary means of communication when managing a project.

Project Culture:

Having drawn up a suitable organisation for the project and agreed the roles and responsibilities of everyone involved, it is important to understand where potential clashes of culture may hinder the project. A common problem is openness – some organisations actively promote openness while others operate on a need-to-know basis and actively suppress information. The project manager cannot assume that all stakeholders will cooperate with the way that he or she wants to run the project. Where a culture clash of this nature exists the project manager must negotiate/agree on a strategy for the dissemination of information across the organisation.

Customer/Supplier Relationship:

In simple terms the customer decides the project goal and the supplier or suppliers fulfil the requirements to enable that goal to be achieved. But it is never that simple. The only way to ensure good communications, and effective resolution of issues, is for the customer and supplier to recognise the responsibilities that each have and to work in partnership to achieve success. Responsibilities may be incorporated into contracts and project plans, but the ultimate success of a project organisation hinges on the willingness of the individuals and the groups of individuals involved to work on a partnership basis. Chapter 9: Team Building addresses this topic.

On large projects there may be many different customer/supplier relationships. The project manager may work for a supplying company delivering to its customer, and a sub-contractor may work as a supplier with the project manager as its customer. In many instances these responsibilities will be enshrined in contract – sometimes in linked contracts – and commercial managers may be involved in monitoring legal implications as the project progresses. But the contract is best left in the filing cabinet unless things start to go seriously wrong. Invoking the contract at every stumbling block will most probably exacerbate the situation and sour relations within the overall project organisation. Reasonable people from all parts of the organisation, working together in a reasonable manner, will have a much better chance of achieving success than business lawyers. If a project ends up in litigation everyone loses.

Project Plans:

All of the above organisational considerations, together with a clearly defined project goal and critical attributes, comprise the core of the project plans. This core provides a solid framework for controlling activities across the entire project organisation, and embraces all the stakeholders. Without this framework the project activities would soon run out of control. The initial work carried out in defining an effective project organisation, and making sure that everyone involved understands how it will function and how they fit in, sets the tone for the cooperation required during the remainder of the project. Diagrams and words are necessary in defining the organisation, but group presentations and one to one conversations are also required to communicate how it is intended to function in practice.

The dynamics of the organisation are discussed further in Chapter 9: Team Building, and in Chapter 10: Controlling the Project. But there is still much to be done in identifying all the detailed project deliverables to be produced, deciding on the work that needs to be done to create these deliverables, and preparing a schedule to facilitate a controlled and measurable progression of the work.

5: Planning

Planning is invariably associated with project management, probably more so than any other project management discipline. There is always a sense of achievement when a Gantt chart or Bar chart is produced at the start of a project. It is satisfying to demonstrate how events will unfold to deliver the anticipated benefits on time and within budget – and it gives all the stakeholders confidence.

But the reason "again" is included in the illustration above is because planning is an ongoing activity during the course of a project, for all but the simplest of undertakings. The original plans will usually be superseded by new plans as the project unfolds, and possibly on more than one occasion. This is realism not pessimism. A plan is a representation of the future, and in project terms this will be a very complex future. Nothing describes the future more accurately than the narrative "uncertain".

Planning at the Formative stage:

High level plans may be drawn up in the formative stage of a project, perhaps as part of the concept or feasibility study. This will set expectations in terms of costs, timescales, scope and quality before sufficient information has been gathered to carry out proper estimating and detailed planning. This may be acceptable for small projects, but for large or complex projects it is necessary to define in more detail what it is that needs to be developed in order to achieve the project goal. This detail is essential if the plans for the project are to have any credibility.

The definition phase of a project is primarily concerned with specifying in detail what needs to be created in order to achieve the project goal. Many different types of specification may be produced, for example technical requirements, functional requirements, operational requirements, outline designs and architectural drawings. The objective of creating these specifications is to understand the product that is to be created in depth, and to agree this understanding with the customer and the end user. The specifications must include sufficient detail to be able recognise the constituent parts of the product and to illustrate how it will function in an operational environment. We are effectively envisioning the future when the project is complete. When we have a clear picture of the product, its constituent parts and its operation, we can then plan in detail the work required to achieve that future. On a large project the definition phase will involve a substantial amount of work, and therefore cost, and a detailed plan will be drawn up to control this work.

Detailed Planning:

When the project is started up "in earnest", that is when authorisation has been given to ramp up the resources and to spend money for the main phases, the original estimates and plans are reviewed and expanded by the project team charged with delivery of the product. There may be a significant disconnect between the initial phase and the project itself for a variety of reasons – some of the problems that may be encountered when a project is put out to tender are discussed in Appendix I: Bid to Project. It may be necessary to draw up new plans, or to add more detail to existing plans, before work can commence.

As the project unfolds progress may deviate from the planned schedule, and if this deviation is significant the current plans may become untenable and a hindrance to proper control. If this situation develops then further changes to the plans will be required – planning is an ongoing activity during the course of a project. This does not necessarily mean that key dates within the plans will be missed, but the means of achieving these dates may differ from original intentions.

We cannot predict the future accurately, especially a complex future that relates to the period of rapid change set in motion by a project – we are just not that clever. What we have to aim for is the best performance possible under the given circumstances, hence the five 'P's.

Proper – Planning – Prevents – Poor – Performance

Without detailed plans for a project we would have only a vague idea of where to start, the dependencies that existed between activities, and the skills and resources required to carry out the work. Diligent planning is rewarded in the longer term – "the more I plan the luckier I get" is often quoted. But project managers should not tinker endlessly with detailed plans and effectively plan themselves to a standstill. If the groundwork has been carried out carefully, and a robust plan has been created that feels about right in relation to the triple constraint, then it is time to get on with the job.

Detailed planning for a project is rarely linear and it is usually necessary to undertake several iterations of the planning process in order to arrive at the best solution. However it is worth looking at the major steps that need to be taken in order to create the familiar Gantt chart, the symbolic culmination of the detailed planning exercise. Henry Gantt is credited with devising this chart, hence the name. Apparently it was first used in a major way by the USA during the First World War. Nowadays it is quite often referred to as a Bar chart.

There are several techniques and structures that can be used to progress the detailed planning of the work in an orderly fashion. The first step is to identify the various components that comprise the product or deliverable of the project and to understand how these components relate to each other.

Product Breakdown Structure (PBS):

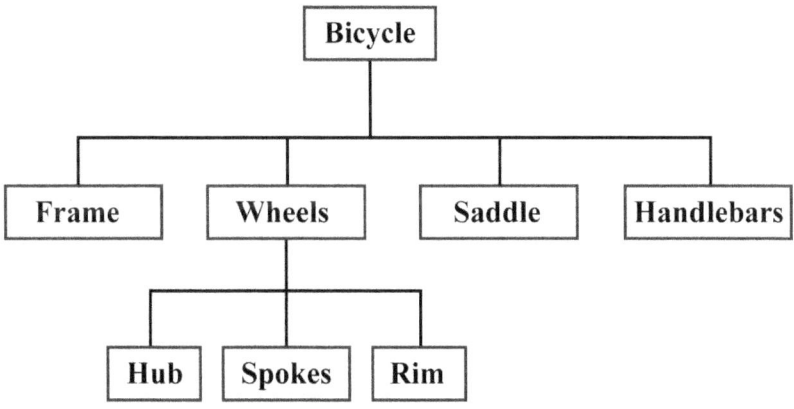

The above is a simplified representation of the individual components that make up a bicycle. It requires little explanation except to point out that it is hierarchical. Components can be further split down into sub-components – in this case the wheels are shown as comprising 3 sub-components. If all the components of a bicycle are included, the PBS for even this modest piece of engineering becomes quite extensive.

For a major undertaking e.g. building of an aircraft or a ship, we can imagine the complexities that need to be represented by this technique – creating a PBS would be a significant project in its own right. But for most projects it is a straightforward and proven technique to aid understanding of what it is that is required to be delivered. For example the subsystems, the component programmes, and the modules of a software development can be quite effectively represented in this manner.

The product breakdown structure generates a list of all the individual components, and the relationships between these components, that need to be produced in order to create the final product – in this case a bicycle. This list can be used as a basis for *configuration management* that will be required where components are developed through a number of iterations or versions. When the finished product requires maintenance during its operation, for example a replacement part, it is essential to know the actual version numbers of the components that have been installed in a finished product. Configuration management of the component parts of a complex product is an essential element in the overall management of information for a project.

When we have established a good understanding of the product to be delivered in terms of its component parts, we can determine the *work* that has to be carried out to create these components. We can also determine the work required to fit these components together to build the product. Work is usually referred to as a task when it has a short duration, for example to write a software module; and it is often referred to as an activity if it occurs over a longer period of time, for example manage the project.

Work Breakdown Structure (WBS):

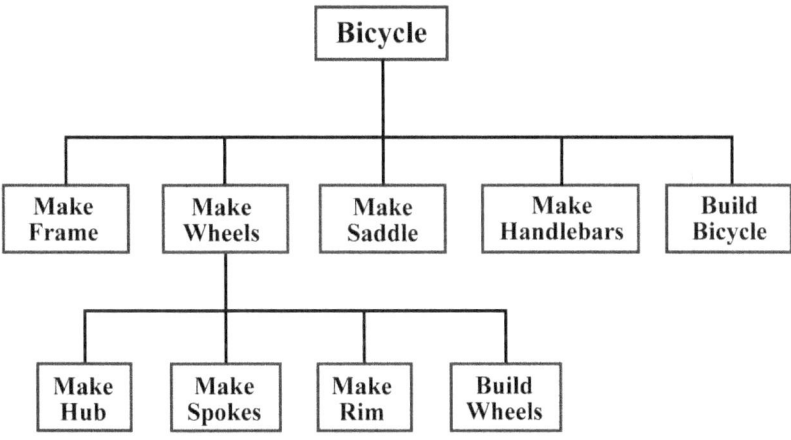

Each box in the above structure represents work that has to be achieved – work that will require human as well as material resources. In addition to making the individual components that were identified in the PBS we will have to fit these together to produce the bicycle. This fitting together is shown at two levels in the example – building the wheels and also building up the complete bicycle.

It is worth reflecting on how quickly the work breakdown structure can develop even more complexity than the PBS, because there are now many new tasks associated with the building process. By generating the WBS in a "top down" manner we are linking together tasks that are logically connected – in our example the making of the components for the wheels, and then fitting them together, are all logically connected. We have effectively created a ***work package*** for the wheels, and this is an important concept in project management.

Development of a large computer system, or a major piece of engineering, cannot be effectively controlled unless we create a team structure based on the work package concept. This enables the project manager to divide the total work of his team into several parts, and to delegate responsibility for each part to a work-package manager, or team leader. The concept and practice of work breakdown structures provides a sound basis for creating an appropriate team structure within the core project team charged with creating the product. Each team has responsibility for making (or acquiring) the individual components associated with this part of the product, for fitting these components together, and for making sure that they operate as required. In our bicycle example this means making (or acquiring) the hub, spokes and rims, building the wheels, and then testing them to ensure that they work properly.

In project management terminology the build activities used in the bicycle example are often referred to as *integration* and the work to ensure that they all work properly as a whole is referred to as *integration testing*. Whether we are delivering an aircraft, a complex computer system or any other product, the effort required to integrate all components into a working whole, and then test they work together as required, will account for a very large part of the project budget. The proportion of the project budget required for integration and testing will tend to increase as the complexity of the end product increases.

A work breakdown structure can be used as the basis for estimating the effort required to create individual components, to integrate the components, to carry out integration testing – and importantly to identify the skills required throughout the process. This will eventually lead to an overall cost for the project when overheads such as management, space, administration, materials etc. are included. Estimating is at the heart of the triple constraint – it is discussed separately in Chapter 6: Estimating.

Task Network & Critical Path:

The next step in the detailed planning process is to identify *dependencies* between the various tasks required to create the product, and to determine the *critical path* for the project. For each task the estimated effort of say 10 man days, and the level of resources to be applied of say 2, are combined in order to calculate an estimated elapsed time of 5 days. Knowing the estimated elapsed time for each task, and the dependencies between tasks, a network diagram can be constructed and the critical path identified.

Tasks: A: make frame, B: make hub, C: make spokes, D: make rim,
        E: build wheel, F: make handlebars, G: make saddle, H: build bicycle

(d) Represent a dependency, but no task

Nodes 1, 2, 3, etc. represent the start and end of each task

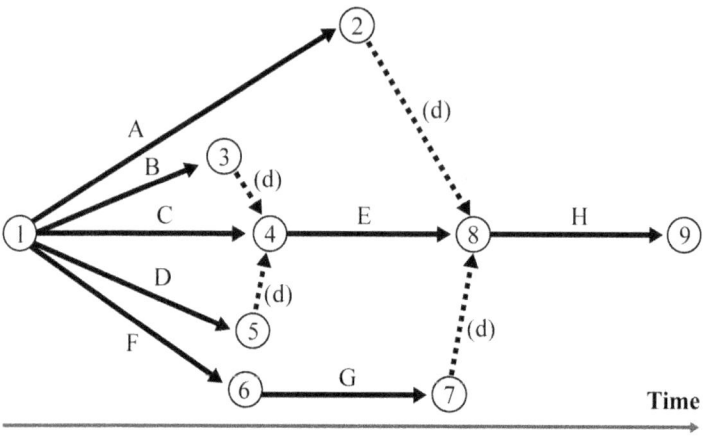

There are several ways of representing tasks and dependencies in diagrammatic form – the technique chosen here for the bicycle example is one of the simplest. The arrows represent the tasks required to deliver each of the components identified in the work breakdown structure. The dependencies have been included in the network – we must make the hub (B), spokes (C) and the rim (D) before we can build the wheels (E), and we need to build the wheels and make all the other components before we can build the bicycle (H).

The dashed lines annotated with (d) are dummy tasks which represent a dependency but with no actual work required – we cannot build the complete bicycle until the wheels and all the other components are ready at node 8. In this particular project the handlebars and the saddle will be made by the same individual and so these tasks are shown as consecutive in the diagram.

In this type of network the length of the arrows represent elapsed time, and this gives a clear picture of the ***critical path*** which runs through tasks C, E and H. This means that there is some slack or "float" in all the other tasks – if they take a little longer than estimated this may not affect the total elapsed time. If an individual task exceeds the estimated elapsed time by more than the float available for that task, then the critical path will change. If the predicted elapsed times are A: 10 days, C: 6 days, E: 8 days, then if A actually requires 15 days the critical path will now run through A and H.

Diagrams of this type, with comprehensive calculations of float, can be created by software applications provided all the tasks, durations and dependencies are supplied. But be aware – these networks can become enormously complex and unwieldy when large numbers of tasks and dependencies are incorporated. Specialist knowledge is necessary to create a practical network in these circumstances. For most projects a reasonable approach is to incorporate the estimated elapsed times for the tasks and the dependencies between them in a Gantt chart – provided of course that these dependencies are clearly understood.

Gantt or Bar Chart:

Tasks

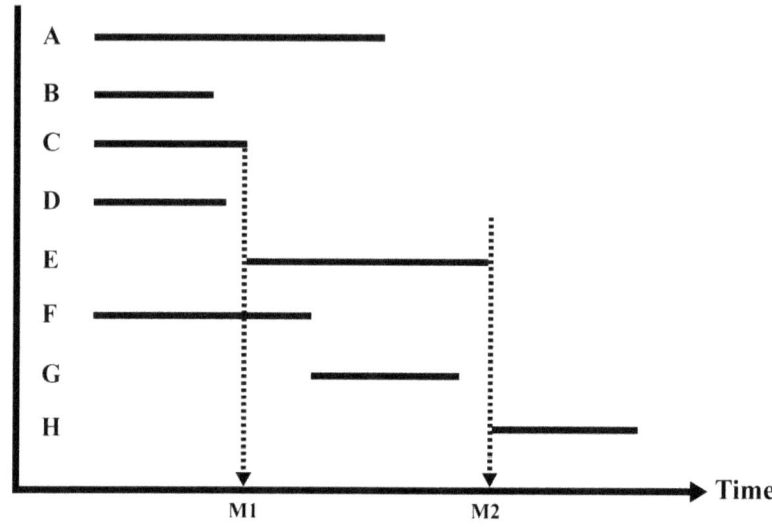

The Gantt chart is a powerful representation of the tasks and activities to be carried out, and also the estimated elapsed time for each individual task. It incorporates the dependencies identified during the network analysis and enables us to highlight milestones – key points in the schedule that represent tangible and measureable progress. In this case M1 indicates that all the components required for the wheels are available and building of the wheels can commence. When M2 is achieved, building of the complete bicycle can begin.

Milestone Plan:

For large projects, with hundreds of activities and tasks, upwards reporting of progress against a detailed Gantt chart is not usually appropriate. Senior managers are primarily interested to know whether or not key elements of the project are being completed according to the plans. To cater for this it is a good idea to generate a separate milestone plan.

The milestone plan depicts the dates within the overall project schedule that are associated with interim deliverables and/or the end of a phase. Milestones signify the completion of a set of activities and tasks that are logically connected, and they can best be defined as "when something has been completed/reached/signed off". There are often distinct streams of milestones, and dependencies between these streams, as in this simplified example of an application software development:

Date	Milestone	When...	Responsibility
31 Jan	M1	plans agreed	project manager
15 Mar	M2	requirements signed-off	customer
30 Apr	M3	design finalised	design authority
30 Apr	M4	acceptance criteria agreed	customer
30 Sep	M5	development complete	project manager
15 Nov	M6	system text complete	design authority
15 Nov	M7	acceptance tests ready	customer
31 Dec	M8	system accepted	customer

This illustration shows two distinct but linked streams of milestones. One stream relates to the development work being carried out – M1, M3, M5 & M6, and the other relates to customer activities – M2, M4, M7 & M8. The primary responsibility for each milestone is shown, but in practice all participants in the project must support each other in achieving the milestones. For example the development team will usually produce the requirements specification after discussion with the customer, but it is the customer's responsibility to agree to it and sign it off in order to achieve the milestone.

Milestones are usually associated with interim deliverables, and the creation of a milestone plan naturally provides a list of these. In the above example the interim deliverables are – requirements specification, design specification, acceptance criteria, developed software and acceptance test scripts.

For very large projects, milestone plans of this nature are an essential aid to interpretation of progress. These can become quite complex and, as for all plans, it is important to strike an appropriate level of detail in constructing a milestone plan. By focussing on the key events senior management will be able to relate better to the progress being made – too many milestones and the main purpose of this plan will be undermined. An added benefit here is that the project manager is keeping the overall high level picture of the project in mind at all times, and this will help him or her in thinking ahead to future events.

Refining the Plans:

As mentioned earlier, the linear depiction of planning outlined here – PBS, WBS, dependencies, Gantt, Milestones – is not possible without estimates of the effort required for the tasks and activities. This is discussed in Chapter 6: Estimating. It is also important to understand the assumptions that are being made with respect to the numbers and availability of resources required to implement the plan.

In practice a considerable amount of trial and error, and analysis of resource levels, will be necessary in order to fit everything together into a sensible Gantt. For projects that are resource intensive, for example large software development projects, *resource smoothing* is essential to keep the team size at a manageable level throughout the project. And it is important to think carefully about the initial resourcing requirements – a gradual build up in the first few weeks of a project usually works best. Attempts to build up the team size too quickly could result in a chaotic and inefficient start to the work.

While developing the plans the project manager should already be thinking about the actual individuals that he or she would like on the team. Either through previous experience, or through contacts, or through the support of senior managers the project manager should aim to populate the team with the very best individuals available for the job in hand. This is equally as important to the success of the project as are realistic estimates and timescales. The difference that an excellent individual can make to a project's progress is very significant, especially in a technical environment.

A Cautionary Tale:

Detailed work breakdown structures with many hierarchical levels, and Gantt charts with hundreds of tasks carefully scheduled over time, may look impressive – but they are not always appropriate. Every time a task is broken down into two or more sub-tasks, a dependency or a relationship is introduced. If there are 2 sub-tasks there is 1 relationship between them; for 3 sub-tasks there are 3 relationships; for 4 sub-tasks there are 6 relationships; for 5 sub-tasks there are 10, and so on. By splitting the task we are breaking up what was originally a cohesive entity into components with dependencies, and this is not always a good idea:

I was assigned as a business analyst – to work with a team of 7 other analysts – during the investigation and specification of the business requirements of a new computer system for a large company. The project manager in charge of this work decided to split the work into small 2 or 3 day tasks and allocate these one at a time to each of the team. Our work involved liaising with the various departments of the company and talking to the end users about their requirements from the proposed system.

The problem was that we all wanted to talk to the same people about different aspects of their department's activities, and then we specified these in isolation from the other aspects – that were of course all related. Apart from making a thorough nuisance of ourselves with the department managers and their staff, we then needed a lot of further discussion and work to create a sensible specification for each business function. The investigation was fragmented and had lost cohesion as a result. This approach was abandoned in favour of broad functional areas of investigation, each area being allocated to one business analyst.

I can understand the project manager's desire to split the work into small tasks, thus enabling close control of our activities, but it was not appropriate under the circumstances. All plans should be constructed with cohesion in mind – this results in more efficient execution when the work is carried out. In the example of the bicycle, we would not divide the task of building the frame into separate sub-tasks for each of the individual frame parts – forks, top tube, down tube, seat tube etc. – and then allocate the making of these to separate individuals. It would not make sense.

At this point it is worth reflecting on the main reason for planning, and the benefits to be gained by doing it properly:

Benefits of Good Planning:

There is no better way to verify that the original objectives of the project are reasonable, and that the timescales and costs predicted are tenable, than to attempt to plan the work in detail. In-depth planning puts some real substance behind the anticipated parameters of the triple constraint – although it may result in a revision of the original predictions.

Planning enables us to determine the most appropriate life cycle for the project and to identify other milestones that will demonstrate real progress when the work is being carried out. Checkpoints are often introduced at the end of each phase of the life cycle, or on achieving a major milestone. At these checkpoints a thorough review of the project may be undertaken before authorisation to continue further is given. These are usually referred to as *gateway reviews*.

A major objective of planning is to analyse the skills required in the project team that will carry out the work. It is crucial to identify these skills as far in advance as possible as they are often in short supply, and specialised skills may be particularly difficult to obtain. If the intention is to form a team and locate all or most of this team in one location, the personnel requirements calculated during the planning stage will naturally lead to a search for the necessary space and equipment.

It is also important to remember that the resources allocated to specific tasks, and at specific times in the planned project schedule, are real people. Real people have holidays, and they have days off work for sickness, training, jury duty and a whole host of other reasons. In the initial planning stages this level of detail for each member of the team cannot be known, so it is essential to allocate a realistic number of available days on a weekly or monthly basis to take absences into account over the longer term.

It is worth remembering also that it is very difficult to achieve the same level of productivity over the Christmas period, and during the long school holidays in the summer, as it is at other times during the year. Some projects may be vulnerable to delays as a result of severe weather conditions during the winter months, and it may be appropriate to allow for this eventuality during planning.

As described in this chapter, the planning process creates a series of models that can be used to construct a schedule of work, a Gantt chart. As the project progresses, achievements against the Gantt can be measured by recording the actual work carried out to date and estimating the work still outstanding. See Chapter 10: Controlling the Project. This will highlight where the work is ahead of or behind schedule and the impact or potential impact on dependencies. There are some very sophisticated software applications available to make this job easier for projects where many tasks, activities and dependencies need to be monitored.

Risk Management:

During the planning phase an assessment of the risks associated with undertaking the project should be carried out and a plan to manage these risks devised. This plan will most probably result in additional tasks or activities that will need to be estimated and incorporated into the overall project schedule. See Chapter 7: Risk Management.

Quality:

As part of the planning process the quality measures to be adopted on the project should be identified together with the work associated with these measures. In determining the total work content of a project and creating a schedule, quality activities and tasks need to be incorporated into the plans. See Chapter 8: Quality Management.

Project Management Plan:

The culmination of all planning activities results in a document – the Project Management Plan (PMP). As a minimum the PMP should include all the information relating to the project goal, the organisation, work breakdown, dependencies, resourcing and schedules, risk and quality management, and change control. It should also include any other relevant information that influences the management of the project, for example contractual terms and conditions. The PMP is a living document, and should be maintained so that it reflects changing circumstances in the management of the project as it progresses.

Planning involves the formulation of detailed estimates for the work to be done, but for the sake of clarity I have avoided this central planning activity until now. Estimating has a major influence on the ability of the project manager to control the work as it is carried out, and also on the perceived success of the project. The next chapter addresses this topic.

6: Estimating

The Heart of Planning:

Estimating is at the heart of planning and it is a continuous process throughout the life cycle of a project. When the project goal is determined initially, estimates are required in order to conduct a cost/benefit analysis and to allocate sufficient budget should the project be authorised. Arriving at a reasoned estimate at this early stage is very challenging since it is almost invariably based on a far less than ideal level of information.

In civil engineering there is a wealth of historical data available that helps to "size" a project in the initial stages by comparing it with recently completed similar projects. There are tried and tested methods to estimate the effort and cost in detail when a work breakdown has been developed, and there are professional estimators who can apply these methods for any given project. Increasingly, however, all projects include a significant element of IT, and this is more problematic.

Over the past few decades there have been several attempts to develop estimating methods for IT projects in general and software developments in particular. These have been based on factors such as the functionality to be incorporated into the system, estimates of the number and size of software components to be developed, the complexity of these components and the complexity of the system overall. But the technology has moved forward rapidly – too rapidly to accumulate a meaningful database of experience from completed projects that could prove useful for predicting future ones.

In the initial phase of a project the only real option is to take a ***top down*** approach to estimating. This can be based on previous experience of similar projects if appropriate, and also on the judgement of experienced managers. Later on, when sufficient detail becomes available to enable the development of a work breakdown structure, estimating of individual tasks can be carried out as part of a ***bottom up*** approach.

There are many separate items that need to be estimated for a project, for example manpower, materials, plant and equipment, office accommodation and computers, overheads and administration. Of these, the manpower costs are becoming increasingly more dominant in most projects. For the remainder of this chapter I will focus on estimates of man effort for low level tasks identified in a WBS, and also on the crucial aspect of obtaining resources with the right skills.

Estimating Work Effort:

It is important to be diligent in all aspects of planning in order to produce a comprehensive and credible schedule of work, usually in the form of a Gantt chart. But if the estimates for the work to be done are inadequate the project is destined to exceed budget and timescales before it has barely got off the ground. Rarely, at least in my own experience, does it turn out that the original estimates have been too high, and sometimes it seems that the definition of an estimate for an individual task is:

"The most optimistic prediction that has a non-zero probability of coming true"

Cost estimates may be optimistic in a situation where winning a bid takes precedence over making a profit on the project. This may occur when a company is aiming to secure follow-on work of greater value, and it may be acceptable to trim profit margins or even to make a loss – but it is unreasonable to apply this optimism to the work effort involved as this will only lead to late delivery.

Estimates that are difficult to achieve are not necessarily unwarranted when the project team is pushing hard to reach a milestone, or are close to the end of a phase within the life cycle. On these occasions there are usually a few make-or-break tasks upon which success will depend and estimates will tend to be driven by deadlines. Overtime and weekend working are quite normal in these situations.

However, optimistic or unrealistic estimates of work effort are not appropriate when estimating all of the work effort involved during the initial detail planning for a project. At this time the definition of an estimate should be:

"A prediction that is equally likely to be above or below the actual result"

When we estimate that a task will take say 5 days, we are making a number of assumptions. We are assuming that the individual who will undertake the task is already suitably skilled to carry it out efficiently. We are also assuming that any support that this individual may require in order to carry out the task is forthcoming at the time it is required. These are general assumptions that are reasonable provided we carry out a proper skills analysis, obtain the right team members, and think about the support that might be required within the team.

When we make estimates as part of planning we should document the assumptions we make in arriving at the estimated values. This has two benefits: it makes us think more rigorously about the estimates in the first instance, and it also provides an audit trail in the event that we need to undertake a re-estimating exercise. Re-estimating some or all of the work outstanding during the course of a large and complex project is not unusual and is important for good project control – see Chapter 10: Controlling the Project. The experience gained as a result of work already completed can be used to enhance the estimates for the work outstanding at any of the regular monitoring and reporting periods, or when a re-estimating exercise is carried out.

Conventional Estimating:

When we estimate we make use of whatever knowledge we have about the particular task or activity in question. We also take account of any experience that we may have of similar tasks or activities. If a body of data exists for work of this nature then it may be applicable to the current project – this type of information is used by professional estimators.

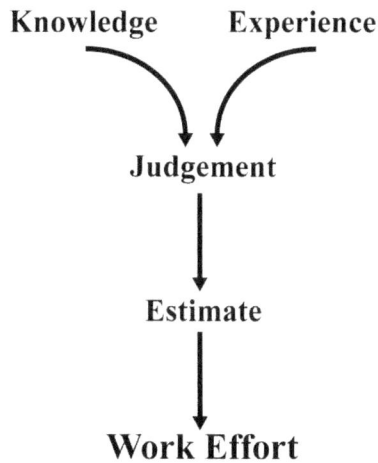

Ultimately we make a judgement in terms of size and complexity and then assign an estimate for the effort required to complete the task, for example a number of man-days. Rather than relying on the judgement of one person it is a good idea to obtain a second opinion.

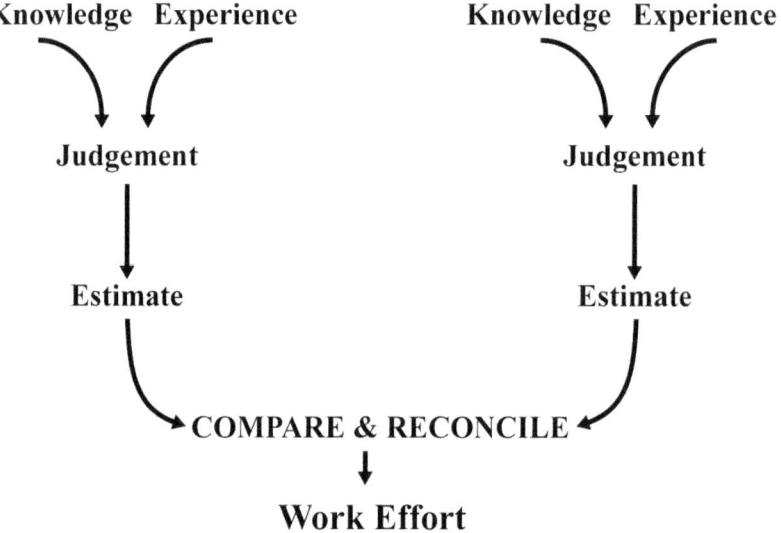

Now we have two independent estimates prepared by two individuals, or by two groups of people, and we can conduct a comparison and reconciliation exercise. This is another occasion when we can use documented assumptions to help arrive at the best possible value for the estimate. All other things being equal, we may decide to take an average of the two separate values to arrive at the final figure. Comparing and reconciling two or more sets of estimates and assumptions can be quite revealing, and provides a more objective view of the judgements that need to be made. The final values resulting from comparison of several independent sets of estimates will increase confidence in the project plans. The cost and time dimensions of the triple constraint are directly related to the estimates for the work to be carried out, emphasising the central role of estimating during the planning exercise.

There will always be considerable uncertainty and risk surrounding the estimates of work on a project, but it is possible to achieve good results under the right circumstances:

I spent a couple of years of my career advising my company's board on the health of a number of large projects ongoing at the time. More often than not our clients demanded fixed price arrangements for system developments and we were acutely aware of the need to be diligent when quoting for the contract. One project in particular stands out as an excellent example of good estimating.

The project objective was to provide a new computer system for the set-up and management of a very large share register for a high street building society. The project to develop, test and implement the new system was based on a fixed price, multi-million pound contract, and timescales were critical.

Major efforts were expended on the work breakdown structure for the system, and on estimating for the software development before signing up to the contract. These efforts paid off and the system was delivered on time and to budget with only a few teething problems. There were many factors that contributed to the success of the project, not least of which was the competence of the project manager and her ability to motivate the team. But having a realistic and carefully constructed set of estimates played a major role in the project's success.

Variations in Performance:

When we estimate as part of project planning, it is unlikely that we will know which individual will be carrying out a particular task – so we are in effect estimating for the averagely efficient person. Later in the project, when we have experience of the team's productivity, we may tailor the estimates for individual team members. Under these circumstances it is usually preferable to ask the individuals concerned to determine the estimate themselves, as this will encourage commitment to complete the work on time.

In a study carried out some years ago by Tom DeMarco and Timothy Lister, a large group of computer programmers (coders) were each given the exact same specification for a medium-sized programme. The resulting software produced by each coder was then subjected to a standard acceptance test until the expected results were achieved. The time taken for each member of the group to write the programme, debug it and arrive at the correct results was measured. The outcome of the study is represented in the diagram below.

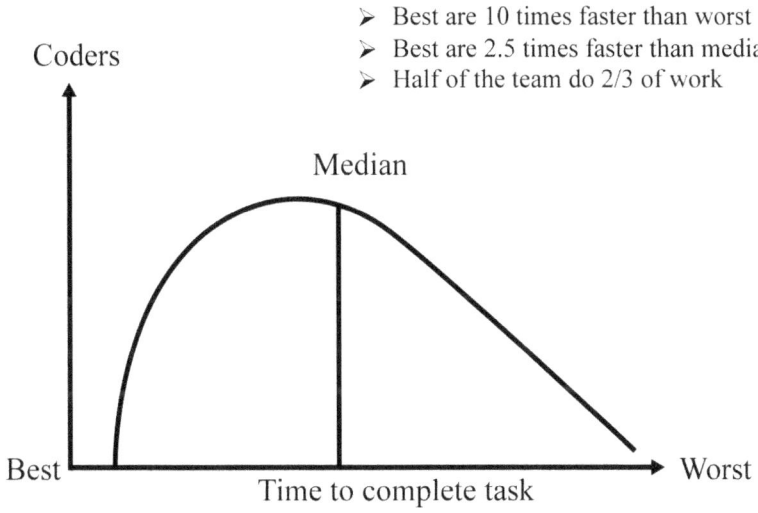

The best coders completed the job quickly and accurately – the worst took up to ten times longer than the best. The chart above shows a general distribution of the times taken by all the coders in the group. I have personally experienced very similar performance variations in the groups of software developers that have been part of project teams I have managed – not just once but on every single occasion when I have managed a software development.

This of course reflects our experiences in many walks of life – some individuals are highly productive at their chosen trade or profession, while others struggle to achieve an average performance. The impact of carrying the least able individuals as part of a project team are not normally factored into the estimates during the initial planning, and this impact can be quite alarming.

Suppose that we have seven similar tasks, and these are each estimated to require ten days of effort. Because of the dependencies in our plan all the tasks must be completed within ten elapsed days, and we decide to use seven members of our project team to carry out these tasks:

7 tasks estimated at 10 days each = 70 man-days

Task	Member	Rating	Days
1	Andrew	Best	3 days
2	Jenny	Best	4 days
3	John	V.Good	5 days
4	Linda	Best	4 days
5	Lindsey	Best	3 days
6	Mark	V.Good	5 days
7	Simon	Worst	46 days

70 man-days in Total

We have been extremely fortunate in that six of the team members are rated as the best, or very good, and they all complete their individual task well within the ten day estimate. Unfortunately the seventh member of the team is one of the least productive and takes ten times longer than most of the others. We still complete the seven tasks in the original 70 man-days of effort that we estimated, but the elapsed time of 46 days is clearly unacceptable. Simon is obviously not sufficiently experienced or capable to do the work he has been allocated, or perhaps his focus is elsewhere.

When carrying out planning for a project we normally estimate for the average individual – in the absence of better information it's the best we can do under the circumstances. It is incumbent upon the project manager, and other stakeholders at management level, to ensure that the project team is properly resourced with the right skills. If the project goal is crucial to the future of the business the aim should be to put the most capable people into the team to give it the best chance of success.

Contingency:

Estimates should never be given more credence than their name implies. Since we obviously cannot forecast the work to be carried out on a project with total confidence, and since we cannot control all the events that might impede the project's progress, we must incorporate contingency into the project plans. And this contingency needs to be applied to each of the three dimensions of the triple constraint.

In terms of the project scope it is inevitable that, except perhaps for very small projects, changes to this scope will occur during the course of the project. Some changes will not be a problem, but others may cause significant difficulties by increasing the scope of work. This problem of *scope creep*, and how to control it, is discussed in Chapter 10: Controlling the Project. In terms of planning, we should include contingency for additional work associated with changes and provide for this in the costing and timescales. It is also very likely that some work will come to light that, although not a change to the agreed scope, was not identified at the initial planning stage. This work may prove essential to the success of the project and contingency should be provided to cover this eventuality.

The project manager needs to be continually aware that the plans are based on estimates, and should err on the side of caution by assuming that overrun will occur on some tasks. He or she also needs to be aware that obtaining all the necessary resources with the right skills and at the right time is not always possible, and this might have an impact on dependencies. The project manager may have identified all the dependencies between the various tasks, and defined the critical path, but things can and usually do change as a project moves forward. If a critical activity is delayed then the project will also be delayed, unless sufficient contingency in the form of "float" has been built into the critical path.

Contingency to cater for scope changes, additional cost and critical path disruption should always be included in the plans from the outset. There are many variables that cannot be foreseen during planning, and a plan without contingency is totally unrealistic. Without contingency the estimated cost will most probably be exceeded and timescales will slip. This will cause a lack of confidence throughout the project team and the wider project organisation. It will result in a drop in morale among those most closely associated with the project, the consequences of which could be considerable.

Contingency allowances belong to the project as a whole – they are not just a personal safety net for the project manager. They should therefore be visible, and the levels of contingency remaining should be monitored and reported as part of the regular progress reporting. Contingency in relation to the work effort of the project team is normally under the control of the project manager, but if it becomes necessary to release some of the contingency from the project budget, the project manager will have to obtain authorisation from senior management.

Inheriting Estimates:

A project manager sometimes inherits a set of estimates that have been prepared prior to his or her involvement in the project. As a priority he or she must establish the provenance of these estimates and also the assumptions that were made when they were originally compiled.

If it is established that they are incomplete or not well founded, the entire project should be re-estimated. Estimates are at the heart of planning and the project manager owns the plans upon which the triple constraint rests. He or she must begin with confidence that the milestones and the product delivery dates are achievable based on the plans.

7: Risk Management

Risks are a normal part of everyday life for all of us, irrespective of our chosen lifestyles. But in the modern world an aversion to risk seems to have resulted in the proliferation of situations where a risk assessment is deemed necessary. In some cases assessments are being carried out before undertaking what are essentially routine activities. This practice has become widespread, to the point where it is interfering with the normal functioning of society. A small industry seems to have emerged to promote the assessment and management of risk. The danger of this trend is that the really significant risks become obscured amongst those of much lesser consequence – and this is something we must guard against when managing a project.

Projects do attract significant risk by their very nature – the introduction of rapid change. As part of the planning process it is important to carry out a risk assessment for the entire project, and then to create a risk management plan comprising actions that are designed to mitigate or eliminate the risks that have been identified. This information is incorporated in a *risk register*, which should be reviewed on a regular basis throughout the project. Provided that the risk management actions are having the desired effect, the risks need only be monitored until they have expired. If a risk is expected to mature despite the current efforts, further actions should be considered to contain it. It is quite likely that new risks will emerge during the course of a project and these will need to be incorporated into the risk register for regular review.

Risk Analysis:

A common form of risk analysis is represented as follows:

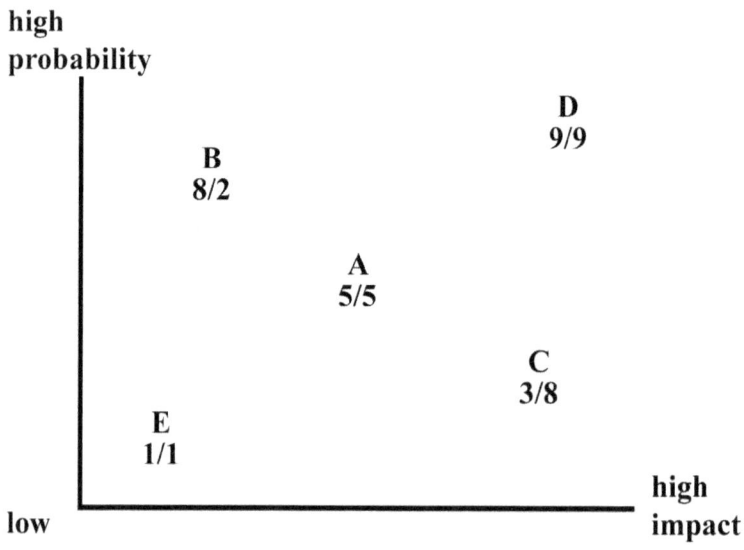

Each risk identified is allocated a probability score and an impact score in the range 1 to 10, where 1 represents a very low probability or impact and 10 represents a very high probability or impact. Risk 'C' has a combined assessment of 3/8 – it has a low probability of occurring but a high impact if it does. Risk 'B' has a combined assessment of 8/2 – it has a high probability of occurring, but with low impact if it does.

Risk Assessment Workshop:

The type of analysis described above is quite straightforward and can be effectively carried out in a workshop environment. However, before conducting a risk assessment workshop it is advisable to put some form of simple structure in place to avoid a disorderly approach to identifying the risks. A topic-based discussion provides discipline that encourages all the attendees to focus their thoughts in one area at the same time, thereby increasing the effectiveness of the workshop. An example of a simple structure is:

Topic	Example
Resources	availability of specialist skills
Commercial	contractual penalties
Technical	performance consideration
External	changes to legislation
Security	official secrets

Environmental   pollution

Health & Safety   mandatory requirements

Other   brainstorm

Risks may arise from any place within the overall context of the project and all major stakeholders should be involved in the identification and evaluation of risks. Each risk should be allocated to a named individual who then takes responsibility for managing the appropriate mitigating actions. The project manager will probably have to manage many of the risks, but some risks will almost certainly be associated with eventualities outside his or her sphere of management control. Some risks will inevitably relate to the stakeholders' immediate environments and these should be owned by the stakeholders concerned. The project manager will maintain the register of all the risks and will be responsible for their regular review throughout the project. This review can take place either during the regular progress meetings or, in the case of large projects, in specific risk management meetings.

Risk Register:

A risk register is a straightforward list of all the key risks identified and associated information. A typical register will include the following:

- ➢ Risk number
- ➢ Risk type (technical, commercial etc.)
- ➢ Description of risk

> ➢ Probability
> ➢ Impact
> ➢ Owner of risk
> ➢ Mitigating actions & effectiveness
> ➢ Status of risk – pending, mature, expired

Dealing with risk costs money and, for large projects in particular, a separate risk mitigation budget may be set aside and drawn down as required during the course of the project. A risk that relates to a future phase of the project and cannot be addressed at the present time will have a status of pending. Some risks may never mature, while others will be mitigated by the management actions and eventually expire.

It is easy to get carried away when assessing risks and to imagine all sorts of problems that could beset the project. The key to producing an effective evaluation of risks is to focus on those with the most potential for jeopardising the project's success. If this results in a significant number of very high risks then we should be questioning the wisdom of undertaking the project in the first place. Risks need to be reviewed on a regular basis in formal meetings, perhaps every two weeks. If the risk register contains a large number of risks the effort and time required to review these can become excessive.

I have witnessed one project with a very large risk register that was totally inappropriate:

During my time as project advisor to our company's board I was directed to evaluate the health of a project we were carrying out in a central government department. This particular project stands out as an example of extreme risk management.

When I first became involved with the project I was invited to attend the regular risk management meeting where I was presented with a copy of a very large risk register. It was quite a complex project, but not particularly large, and I wondered how it could have attracted so much risk. The meeting was attended by about 10 people, and we sat through the entire morning and part of the afternoon reviewing each risk in turn.

After sometimes quite lengthy discussion of an individual risk, the value assigned to it might be deemed to have changed from say 7/4 to 6/4. It was a long and tortuous process and I was relieved when it was over. These large and protracted risk meetings are a waste of time – time that would be much better spent in resolving issues and encouraging the forward momentum of the project. If the owner of a risk is confident that it is being managed effectively, there is little value in debating at length the actual values assigned to it.

It is important to use common sense and to keep a sense of proportion when considering the risks to a project. If a project is worthwhile and apparently feasible, we should be focussing on the genuine risks, not wasting energy on imagined risk. Genuine risks need to be met head-on, because in my experience these risks will never go away. And if we don't **actively attack** these risks then one day they will actively attack the project.

Project Managers and Risk:

Single handed sailors who cross oceans in small boats are taking great risks. But they do everything in their power to mitigate the dangers through careful preparation of their boat, provisioning for the voyage and spending long hours studying navigation charts and nautical almanacs. But it is overcoming the challenges they encounter during their ocean passage that seems to give them the most satisfaction.

The project equivalent is careful organising, diligent estimating and planning, risk assessment and providing a suitable work environment for the team. This gives confidence that everything possible has been done initially to achieve success, and from then on the project manager must use his or her wits on a daily basis to keep the project on course. Risk aversion is an admirable trait when crossing a busy road or a railway track, but it does not sit comfortably with the management of rapid change. In my experience the most successful project managers are those who feel reasonably comfortable with risk and uncertainty, and perhaps even relish it from time to time.

8: Quality Management

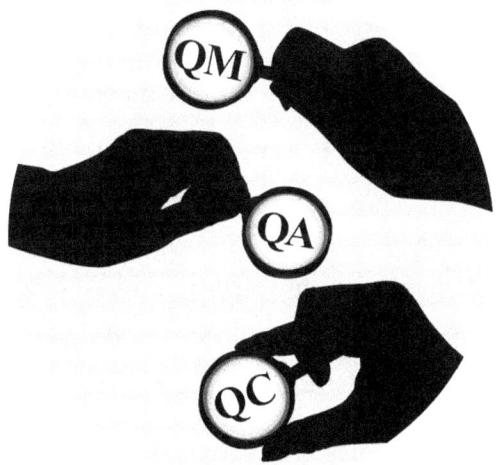

What is Quality?

Quality is an essential ingredient in every project otherwise the critical attributes of the project goal will not be achieved. But that does not necessarily mean that the product of the project has to be of high quality. A Volkswagen car is of good quality, but compared to say a Rolls Royce it is not of high quality. Both vehicles provide what their customer base wants – a vehicle that is fit for their particular purpose – and both are of good quality. While both vehicles may be solid and reliable, the Rolls Royce is a luxury car and of very high quality.

In determining what quality means in respect of a particular project, the primary input must come for the customer and the end user of the product. Is it basic function that is required or are additional "nice to have" features to be incorporated? It can be a difficult balancing act because it is often these additional features that make the product attractive, and give the project more credibility. On the other hand the main driving force for the project may be based on business critical considerations that are time dependent, and attractive features that require additional time are not relevant. The meaning of quality that applies to a particular project must be determined when the project goal and critical attributes are defined, and this quality must be incorporated into the scope & quality baseline of the triple constraint as this represents all the work that has to be carried out.

Quality Management System:

Most companies have developed a Quality Management System *(QMS)* that describes the standards and processes to be carried out during the course of conducting their business. These standards and processes are normally embodied within the company's *Quality Manual (QM)*, and will cover aspects of the business such as documentation standards, documentation control, validation processes, authorisation and criteria for acceptance of developed products. The level of detail incorporated in the QM varies significantly from one company to another.

In project terms, quality management begins with the QMS used by the customer and/or the supplier, either of which may mandate the application of a Project Management Methodology. It is not uncommon on large projects, involving several companies, for aspects from several methodologies to be incorporated within the overarching project organisation. It is the project manager's responsibility to ensure that the quality processes used across the entire project are understood, agreed and put into practice. Change Control and Risk Management are examples of standard processes that might be mandated for all companies involved in a large project.

Quality Assurance:

Quality Assurance *(QA)* is the expression normally used to describe the processes aimed at preventing mistakes and therefore achieving the quality requirements of the company. Testing constituent parts of a product, and the complete product itself, during the course of a project is the mainstay of Quality Assurance. There are likely to be several separate stages of testing applied during the development of a product, each successive stage comprising greater integration of the components produced during the course of the project. For a computer system this might comprise programme testing, sub-system testing, system testing, integration and acceptance testing. These different levels of testing contribute progressively to the quality of the final product.

Suppliers will have quality processes relating to testing of products and deliverables to ensure that they meet the technical design criteria and the customer's requirements. Customers should also have quality processes for testing that the delivered products are fit for the purpose intended, and can be successfully integrated into the wider context of their existing business. In large and complex projects supplier testing, customer testing and integration testing will feature significantly in the project plans, and will account for a large proportion of the overall work content and cost of the project.

Quality Control:

In addition to catering for QA activities, the project plans should incorporate activities for detailed inspection of the documentation and the components produced during the course of the project. The expression normally used to describe this inspection technique is Quality Control *(QC)*. Inspections are aimed at ensuring alignment with the overall project scope and conformance to the appropriate standards, for example the format of documentation, coding standards for software, quality of raw materials. Projects create many documents including interim deliverables such as requirements specifications, design drawings and test plans. A common Quality Control technique applied in system development projects is outlined below:

> A member of the project team creates a specification
> The specification is distributed to one or more reviewers
> The reviewers inspect the specification and record their comments and queries. These are copied to the originator of the specification, the other reviewers and a quality recorder
> The quality recorder convenes and chairs a meeting with the originator and the reviewers to discuss the

comments raised and to agree on changes to the specification

> The originator makes the agreed changes to the specification and distributes the revised version

> If the revised specification is agreed, it is signed off by the reviewers

> The list of reviewer comments and the changes arising from these are then filed as a record that the quality control process has been carried out

The reviewers involved in the quality control process should be chosen carefully, and will normally include the individual or team with overall responsibility for the design of the system under development – the design authority. Other reviewers should be members of the team working on parts of the system that are closely related to the specification that is under review.

Quality Audits:

In addition to the quality assurance and quality control activities which are fundamental to the day to day work of the project team, external Quality Audits may be carried out from time to time. These audits may be timed to coincide with the end of one phase of the project and the start of the next. They may be carried out by the internal quality function within a company or by external quality inspectors. On large and complex projects a quality manager may be assigned to the project with responsibility for the supervision of all quality matters.

Basic Quality:

The most basic quality requirement for every project is the creation of documentation that describes the functioning of the final product produced and its constituent parts. This information is essential for the product's support and maintenance in an operational environment. Every company I have worked with has adopted at least this basic level of quality, with one exception:

I signed a two year contract with a large oil company based in Tripoli, Libya, to support all their IT systems. I had many interesting experiences in that country – one of which related to the problems of supporting IT systems without the benefit of any documentation. Colonel Gaddafi had decided to grab 51% of all foreign oil companies and this particular company, which was American owned, decided to pull out altogether. Exit the American IT team – enter the UK IT team.

But where was the documentation? Whether any documentation had ever existed or not we would never know – but we were faced with maintaining the systems of a very large company without it. The only option open to us was to print out all the computer programme coded instructions, and try to work out what these programmes were actually doing.

Our first priority was to get to grips with the expatriate payroll system – otherwise we would not be getting paid for our efforts. We succeeded in getting it up and running, but there was always a lot of finger crossing at the end of each month when the payroll was run. Another major worry was the state of the room where all the magnetic media was stored. Yes, it was air-conditioned, but the AC machines contrived to suck in large quantities of dust and sand in the process.

We did succeed in keeping all of the IT systems running and we also managed to make some improvements to these systems. But the lack of quality measures in the company made for a particularly difficult work assignment in a country where day-to-day existence was already quite challenging.

All quality activities should be identified during the early stages of a project and embedded within the detailed plans when these are developed. The project manager must lead by example when it comes to the team's attitude towards quality. The objective is to instil a sense of pride in the team as a whole that what they are creating is going to be recognised as a very good product – one that is fit for purpose. The pleasure of knowing that you have been part of a successful project lasts for many years after its conclusion.

9: Team Building

Come join my team!

A great deal of human endeavour is carried out by groups of people working together in teams. There are many examples in the field of sports such as football teams, hockey teams and cycling teams. Some sports are played individually such as tennis and golf, but at professional level these sportsmen and women are supported by backroom staff – coaches, nutritionists, physiotherapists etc. all working as a team to help generate the best performance. Medical staff work in teams to support patients in hospitals and in commercial organisations there are teams for specific functions such sales, production and accounting.

All these teams change over time, but rarely do they have to form as quickly as the teams assembled to undertake projects. Good teamwork is essential for project success, but competent teams don't just appear and effective teamwork doesn't just happen. Individual team members must be sought out and then built into a team specifically to undertake the project.

In the early stages of a project a small team is usually formed, either to carry out a feasibility/concept study, or to prepare a commercial bid for the project in response to an invitation to tender. This team will carry out some estimating and planning, and in the case of a commercial bid this will be quite detailed. If the project is subsequently approved, a project manager will be appointed to develop or refine the detailed plans and to deliver the project. The initial team may or may not continue to be involved with the project in the phases that follow.

The effectiveness of transition from planning to actively doing the work will depend to a large extent on securing resources with the appropriate skills, and assembling them into a cohesive team. Cohesion is the central issue here – it is important to remember that we are combining resources in a *novel* way to undertake a *unique* scope of work, and we are doing this very rapidly. Many of the team members will never have worked together before and many will be meeting each other for the first time. Working in a project environment might be a completely new experience for some members of the team.

Encouraging Teamwork:

During the start-up process it is the project manager's responsibility to ensure that the entire team, including all stakeholders, appreciate the overall project objectives. Everyone involved must understand their own individual contribution and its importance in achieving project success. Start-up activities, for example presentations and workshops, should be carried out to facilitate the transition from planning to full operation of the project. For large projects it is a good idea to provide an ***induction pack*** for all new joiners. This can explain the overall project objectives and organisation, the background to their own assignment and the processes that will be used on the project, for example project administration and the timing of regular meetings.

Above all the project manager must obtain the best resources for the job in hand. In Chapter 6 we had an example of how much better some coders are than the average person – and the same is true whatever type of role is being carried out. Good team leaders and work-package managers will manage their teams effectively and get the best out of them. Every project needs a good proportion of team members of above average competence; otherwise the project manager will struggle to build momentum and to make good progress against the plans.

During the build-up of resources the project manager must ensure that each new team member understands his or her responsibilities and takes them seriously. It is important to introduce each new member to the rest of the team, and to encourage the establishment of relationships with those in the team who will support or otherwise influence their productivity. For junior members of the team it may be advisable to assign a mentor.

It is motivating to have the project goal represented in some way that is visible to all the team. This might take the form of a model, or a display of pictures, or even just some diagrams – something that encapsulates the purpose of the work that the team are doing and that everyone can relate to. As the project progresses, anything that represents an achievement should be displayed as evidence that progress is being made. A countdown chart for the next major milestone may also be appropriate. Prototypes and demonstration systems are particularly popular and motivating for everyone involved with the project.

The project manager will spend a lot of time attending meetings, visiting the customer and talking to stakeholders and suppliers. There may also be site visits to make. Whenever appropriate the project manager should take the opportunity to involve individual members of the team in these activities. This enhances their overall appreciation of the project and its organisation and it gives them a welcome break from normal routine.

The Problem with People:

In order to become effective a project team needs to gel – team members need to get on together. The reason that this is so important in a project environment is because of the eventual requirement to integrate all the components created by various team members. During the planning phase the work is broken down into manageable chunks – activities and tasks that can be easily measured – but the end product of the project will be an integrated whole of some description. The foundations for successful integration are laid down when the team members have established mutual respect in their relationships and support each other as a matter of course. This level of cooperation leads to early resolution of problems and smoother integration of the components further down the line.

Establishing effective relationships between even a few individuals is not always straightforward, and as the project team grows the number of relationships will proliferate. This can cause problems.

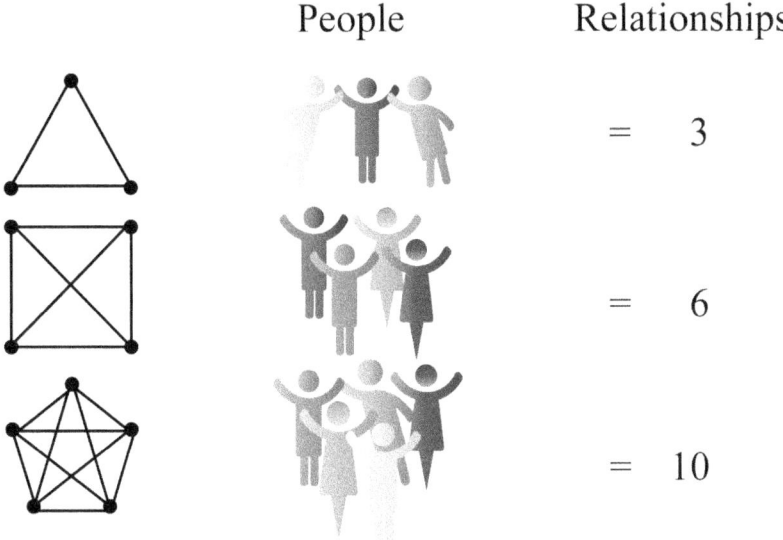

	People	Relationships	
		=	3
		=	6
		=	10

In the example above we begin with 3 team members on the project and this gives rise to 3 relationships. When we add a 4th member to the team, the number of relationships doubles to 6. Adding a 5th member increases this number to 10. Just by adding 2 new members to the team we have more than tripled the number of relationships, and therefore the potential for personalities to clash.

In a project environment comprising 20 people, perhaps 15 in the team carrying out the core work and another 5 in the wider project context, the number of relationships increases to nearly 200. The scope for personality clashes that could hinder communications and co-operation is now enormous. Of course not all of these relationships need to be effective to promote success, but many specific relationships are absolutely crucial in building a cohesive team and maintaining momentum on the project.

This may sound somewhat negative, especially since the whole aim of team building is to promote team spirit with everyone pulling together. But this is not a 3 day team building exercise, it is real life, and I have experienced personality conflicts on every project that I have worked on or managed. The project manager needs to be alert to any problems of this nature and resolve them quickly – good communications and co-operation are the essence of good productivity in a project environment, and those who cannot get on with each other will hinder progress. If a problem situation cannot be resolved by reasonable means then at least one individual will need to be replaced – planning is done on the basis of cohesion within the team, not conflict.

Leadership:

A lot has been written about leadership and different leadership styles. Apart from some obvious characteristics, such as the ability to make tough decisions, there are no hard and fast requirements for project managers. In the armed forces people are told what to do and they do it; in a creative design team people do what they like. Most projects in the commercial world are conducted somewhere between these two extremes. Some project managers claim to adopt different styles of leadership depending upon the situations that arise. Fine if this works, but if it appears to be contrived it will not go down well with the team. Whatever feels natural to the project manager will appear natural to the team, and will doubtless be most effective.

A project manager needs to demonstrate decisiveness. There are lots of activities going on in a busy project environment, and one of the manager's main responsibilities is to make decisions confidently and deal quickly with issues that might hinder the project's forward momentum. There will be times when the team will have to be motivated to put in extra effort in order to meet a forthcoming milestone. If the project manager has been successful in aligning the team with the project goal, it will be much easier to secure this extra effort.

It is important to demonstrate to team members that they are trusted with the work they have been given to do. In my experience the best way to do this is to listen to their concerns, do what you can to smooth their way and then let them get on with it. Team members appreciate being trusted and they also appreciate openness from the project manager; openness allays any suspicions that they are being kept in the dark about important issues. And openness makes the project manager's job easier too – if you always tell the truth you don't have to remember what you said, and to whom you said it. In a complex project environment the last thing the project manager needs is a lot of unnecessary mental clutter.

Management:

Project managers often have a technical background that relates to the project they are responsible for. This can be very helpful in understanding the technical issues that may arise during the course of the project. But it can also be a dangerous distraction for the project manager to get too deeply involved personally in technical issues – he or she must concentrate on keeping the momentum going across the whole project. If an issue arises that is really serious, and a potential show-stopper, the project manager may have to take direct responsibility for its resolution.

The size of project teams varies a lot, from a handful of people up to several hundred or even more. The project manager – or in the case of a very large project the project management team – has to deal with the wider project context in addition to managing those who are actively engaged in developing the product. This wider context may be very complex and include multiple stakeholders, suppliers, legal bodies, trade unions etc. in addition to the customer. For this reason the project manager should have only a limited number of direct reports from within the team.

The capacity of individuals to directly manage others varies considerably, but beyond 5 or 6 direct reports the project manager will have difficulty in servicing all their needs. On larger projects there is likely to be a formal team structure that includes several team leaders or work-package managers. The project manager must be able to trust these individuals to manage their teams effectively and to work professionally with others in a similar position. Lack of communication or cooperation between work-package managers is potentially very damaging in respect of integration activities.

It is quite likely that one or more members of the team will struggle to meet the level of efficiency required to fulfil the tasks allocated to them. It is also possible that one or more members of the team are high-maintenance, in the sense that they are always complaining and using up management time on matters that are of no particular significance. If a team member cannot pull their weight, or if they cannot align themselves with the project goal, or if they are obviously unsettled in their current post, it will be best for all concerned to replace them on the project. Inefficient and high-maintenance individuals are not factored into project plans. These situations will of course have to be managed sensitively.

There are two golden rules for project managers – don't attempt to do any of the tasks that are in the plan (other than manage the project) and don't have too many members of the team as direct reports. Apart from these two rules there is nothing distinctive in the style of management required in a project context. It is the same for management as it is for leadership – the style should be whatever comes most naturally to the project manager.

The project manager must ensure that the team have a suitable environment in which to carry out their work. Noisy offices can be a major distraction, especially for those team members engaged in highly technical tasks that require concentration for long periods at a time. Telephones can also be a major distraction. If a person is deeply engrossed in a challenging mental task when the phone rings, it may take 10 or more minutes to recover to the mental high that existed before the interruption. There should also be quiet areas or rooms for ad hoc and scheduled meetings to be conducted.

The project manager must take the lead in promoting continuous discussion among team members – by actively directing them to discuss particular topics together and by mingling regularly with everyone in the team. Relying on emails for communications does absolutely nothing to promote team spirit and cohesion.

Socialising:

Socialising is an effective way of encouraging good relationships between all those involved in a project, especially in the early stages. It is particularly effective after a project meeting or presentation that has communicated the project status. The main topics and issues will already have been raised and these can be discussed in a more relaxed atmosphere over a drink or a meal. It is an opportunity for stakeholders from across the wider project environment to get involved with the core team, and also for individual team members to express their ideas and concerns.

Some projects organise events such as paint-balling, bowling or go-kart racing. These are generally popular and generate healthy competition, and they are likely to continue as a lively topic of conversation in the days and weeks that follow. They are particularly appropriate for lengthy projects. Celebratory drinks or a meal associated with an important event on the project, perhaps the achievement of a major milestone, are also popular.

Socialising may be less appropriate during the End Game discussed in Chapter 11. At this time workloads and stress levels are likely to be particularly high and the team will be focussed on getting the job finished. Social events outside of work will be seen as a distraction, especially for those with young families or other commitments. They could be viewed as an unwelcome "obligation" by some members of the team.

Some teams work much better than others – here is a tale of two teams:

Team A was responsible for the development, testing and deployment of a new billing system for one of the world's leading express delivery companies. The system was designed for use in over 50 countries in Europe and Africa. As project manager I had responsibility for six separate work packages, including contract management of a £1 million fixed price development carried out by a Dutch company.

The project was resourced with the client's own employees, three consultancies, two software development companies and several freelance contractors. The resulting system was tested and accepted by the client's representatives from six different countries prior to deployment. For many of the team there was a considerable amount of travelling and long periods of working away from home.

There was occasional tension between various groups in the team, but overall everyone worked extremely well together, and most joined in the regular social events that were organised. The whole project ethos was based around a "we can do it" outlook, which in many ways reflected the client's business resolve to deliver all its packages on time. It was a good project, and it was a pleasure to work with positive people from several different companies and countries.

Team B was responsible for the development and testing of a core system for a local council. Although the project team was housed in the council offices there was very little interaction between the team members and the client employees. Virtually all communication was formal and there were no joint social events.

As the development progressed I approached the client management to arrange for their involvement in testing and accepting the system – a normal final phase for a project of this nature. They refused to take any responsibility, stating that it was our obligation to ensure that the system met the agreed requirements. It was a frustrating project in many respects and a cheerless experience overall.

Openness:

If there are no reported problems on a project then it is almost certainly in trouble. At any one time, particularly on a large project, there are likely to be several serious issues that require urgent attention – that is the nature of projects. In many cases these issues will need to be resolved with help from senior management in the companies involved with the project. The important ingredient here is openness.

The manner in which a project team reports and reacts to problems gives a good indication of the general health of the project team. Issues, large or small, need to be tackled head on, and quickly, in order to reduce their impact on forward progress. Everyone involved with the project should be encouraged to be open about the problems they are encountering and to seek help in finding a solution. If this does not happen, the problems and issues will fester and become more difficult to resolve further down the line.

The project manager must take the lead in promoting openness throughout the project environment. He or she should feel comfortable in "telling it as it is" to everyone in the organisation, whatever their seniority. This does not mean being undiplomatic, but there is only one status that applies to a project at any one point in time, and it is the project manager's responsibility to be able to express that status in concise terms.

A healthy project team will see the problems encountered as just another challenge, a normal part of project work, another obstacle to overcome in order to get the job done. A serious problem in one area of the project is a serious problem for everyone involved with the project. Those tasked with resolving the problem should expect and receive the support they require from other members of the team. Success for the project means success for everyone involved – failure likewise.

10: Controlling the Project

Defining the project goal, setting up the organisation, and planning out in detail the work to be done is usually carried out in a relatively calm atmosphere. But this will quickly be replaced by an urgency to make progress against the plans as the team size increases and the work gains momentum. The project manager must now direct and control this hive of activity – especially as it will be consuming large quantities of money.

For even a relatively small team of say 10 software engineers, each costing on average £500 per day, the total cost of the team will amount to £25,000 per week. That equates to £100,000 per month. A team of 10 software developers is not particularly large, but £100,000 is a great deal of money to spend each and every month. It may take some time for the project team to build, but control disciplines must be introduced from day one of the plans.

The most effective means of keeping control of the project is through diligence and consistent measuring of progress. This is accomplished by introducing a regular *drumbeat* into the project environment. The drumbeat involves measuring the effort expended by the team, measuring the progress that is being made against the plans, and communicating the status of the project – normally on a weekly and/or monthly basis. Without the disciplines associated with the drumbeat the project manager will quickly lose control of the project.

Measurement of Work Done:

The first measurement is taken to establish and record the actual work that has been carried out during the reporting period, and from this to calculate the actual work done for the project to date. This can be achieved by team members recording the work they have carried out against individual tasks every reporting period. The actual work done to date for each task may exceed, or fall short of, the work that was planned to be done depending on the availability of the team member who was allocated the task. By accumulating this information across all tasks and activities we can determine how resourcing against the plans is progressing overall.

> ➢ If the work done exceeds the work planned, the project has been over-resourced up to this point in time
> ➢ If the work done is less than the work planned, the project has been under-resourced to this point in time

Small variations in resourcing may not be important – perhaps the result of holidays, training, sickness etc. Large variations in resourcing over several reporting periods indicate a significant underlying problem and will need to be addressed.

By regularly measuring all the work carried out on the project, and accounting for material, overhead and any other costs incurred, we can calculate the total cost of the project up to the end of each reporting period.

Estimates of Work Outstanding:

This important measurement needs to be taken on a regular basis. We can measure the work outstanding at an activity or task level and add it all up to obtain an overall figure of outstanding effort for the project.

The estimated value for outstanding work needs to be carefully considered. For example, if 4 days of work have been carried out during the period on a particular task that was originally estimated at 10 days, we cannot assume that there are 6 days of work outstanding. There may be 3 or 8 days of effort, or some other number of days, still required to finish the task.

Each team member should be asked to re-estimate what is outstanding on the task(s) they have in hand at each reporting period. If they have future tasks on their individual schedule that are very similar to those in hand, it may be appropriate to re-estimate these at the same time based on current experience.

The work outstanding for the remainder of the entire project, plus other material and overhead costs anticipated, will enable a calculation of the estimated total cost to complete the project. Together with the cost of the project to date, the estimated cost to complete will provide a total estimated cost at completion. This total provides a periodic comparison with the cost dimension of the triple constraint as the project progresses.

Measurement of Achievement:

Recording the estimates of outstanding work also enables us to calculate the work *achieved* in a reporting period, as well as for the project to date. This is a very significant figure. The work achieved is a measure of how much the work outstanding has been reduced by, irrespective of how much work has actually been carried out.

For example, if 4 days of work have been carried out on a particular task that was originally estimated at 10 days, and the estimate for the work outstanding is now 8 days, then work actually achieved is only 2 days – the number of days by which the work outstanding has been reduced. This is less than was anticipated in the plans. If the estimate for the work outstanding is now 3 days then the work actually achieved is 7 days, and this is greater than was anticipated in the plans. The work achieved may exceed or fall short of the work actually done for individual tasks and also for the total work done on the project.

> ➤ If the total work done to date exceeds the total work achieved, the project is under-performing against estimates at this point in time
> ➤ If the total work done to date is less than the total work achieved, the project is beating estimates at this point in time

Small variations in achievement may not be significant, but if there is a trend of under-performance against estimates over several periods the project may be in difficulty.

Impact on Timescales:

Consideration of total work done and total work achieved gives an indication of the likely impact on the time dimension of the triple constraint, for example:

> ➤ If the project has been resourced according to the plans, and the work achieved is progressing as anticipated, the project is on schedule

> ➤ If the project has been under-resourced according to the plans, and the work achieved is less than anticipated, the project is falling behind schedule
> ➤ If the project has been resourced according to the plans, but the work achieved is less than anticipated, the project is falling behind schedule
> ➤ If the project has been under-resourced according to the plans, but the work achieved is greater than anticipated, there will be a trade-off in terms of the schedule
> ➤ If the project has been over-resourced according to the plans, but the work achieved is less than anticipated, there will be a trade-off in terms of the schedule

Minor differences may not be significant, but it is important to interpret the figures in terms of their impact on the critical path. The total figures may indicate that the project is on or ahead of schedule, but individual tasks that are on the critical path may be behind schedule. If the float available on a task that is on the critical path is used up or exceeded, the project end date is at risk.

Each time we record the actual work done and the estimated work outstanding we are taking a snap-shot at a particular point in time, and we should be careful not to read too much into the results for a single reporting period. Trends are likely to develop over the course of a project and these will indicate whether or not the project is being properly resourced, and where areas of work have been over or under estimated. We can anticipate that some tasks undertaken early in the project schedule may take a bit longer than similar tasks later in the project – this is quite likely due to initial teething problems and the learning curve for the team.

Interpreting Achievement at Task Level:

Obtaining estimates of the work outstanding for each task is obviously essential to feed into the project control process, but how much confidence should the project manager have in the individual figures provided?

> ➤ the original estimate for a task was 10 days, and 4 days have been worked to date
> ➤ the estimate given by the team member to complete the task is 8 days
> ➤ therefore only 2 days out of the original 10 days have been achieved
> ➤ if it takes 4 days of actual work to achieve 2 days progress against the estimate, could it take another 16 days to achieve the remaining 8 days?

This conclusion would obviously be pessimistic, but it is not necessarily inappropriate – a lot depends on the confidence that the project manager or work-package manager has in this individual. Perhaps the original estimate of 10 days was simply insufficient, but if this particular task is critical for maintaining momentum within the team the project manager has to consider some options:

➢ incentivise the team member to work evenings and weekends in order to complete the task as soon as possible

➢ transfer the task to another team member known to be very fast and accurate

➢ if practical, split the task up and share it with another member of the team

A common problem in many circumstances, and especially in software development projects, is the 90% complete syndrome. A team member may think that the task is just about finished – just a few more tests and it will be fine – but then discovers an issue that is very complex and requires a significant amount of time to resolve. Some tasks can remain at 90% complete for a very long time.

Increasing Resources:

When a project slips significantly behind schedule there may be a knee jerk reaction to throw more resources at the problem. This may or may not be appropriate depending upon the type of project and the particular circumstances. If new resources are introduced into a complex technical environment, they will need support before becoming productive. This support will inevitably have to come from existing members of the team, thus reducing the team's overall productivity. Before embarking on major remedial action in an attempt to bring the project back on schedule, it is essential to understand all the underlying reasons, and the immediate circumstances, surrounding the lack of planned progress.

Techniques and Tools:

There are techniques and software tools that formalise the regular recording and calculations required to review progress against cost and time. Specialised software applications are very useful on large projects, but for smaller projects a spread sheet is usually more appropriate. A commonly used technique is called ***Earned Value*** which is described in Appendix IV.

The value of the information that can be obtained from any technique that aims to forecast project outcomes against cost and time depends primarily on the quality of the estimates. This is the case when initial planning is carried out and it is equally true when estimating the work outstanding at each reporting period. We always return to the heart of planning as discussed in Chapter 6: Estimating.

All the usual clichés apply when reviewing the status of a project at each reporting period: we are where we are; we cannot change the past; we can influence the future. The project manager needs to learn from experience on the project thus far, and quickly, but must then focus on what still needs to be done and how best to achieve it.

Progress Reporting:

The frequency, content and level of information to be included in progress reports will depend upon the complexity of the project, the project organisation established initially, and the specific requirements of the stakeholders. Ideally the project manager would produce only one report for all involved and thereby reduce the possibility of communication issues arising. However, this will not be appropriate on a very large project and the information will need to be summarised for senior management. In addition, there may be sensitive information that a supplier company reports for internal purposes only and this would not be included in the progress report issued to the customer.

When all the relevant numbers relating to work done, work outstanding and work achieved have been established they can be summarised to present an overall picture in the progress report. The project manager must interpret these numbers and express their meaning in the context of overall progress, and in terms that can be understood by senior management. A description of the current activities on the project may be included in the report in the following form:

> ➢ Planned work done during the period, including milestones achieved
> ➢ Planned work not done during the period, including milestones not achieved
> ➢ Unplanned work done during the period
> ➢ Planned work for the next reporting period, including milestones to be achieved

Information expressed in this way gives a clear account of what is currently going on in the project and can be followed through every reporting period. This aids understanding for those at a senior level and those in the wider project context.

Progress report should contain a list of the main issues and the actions in hand to resolve them; they should also contain a list of the main risks together with an appraisal of their implications.

Progress Meetings:

Meetings for the team or teams engaged in the product development work should be held weekly or at least every two weeks. Regular meetings give the project manager an opportunity to communicate progress to everyone on the core team at the same time, and also provide a forum for individuals to put forward concerns and suggestions to improve productivity.

Formal progress meetings with stakeholders and senior management should be held at least monthly. A chair person should be nominated and an agenda circulated prior to the meeting. Minutes should be taken to record decisions made and action points raised, and these should be circulated immediately after the meeting (not just before the next one!)

At these meetings the project manager will normally present the progress report and explain the progress that has been achieved against the plans. The meeting is an opportunity for the project manager to highlight areas where support from the wider project environment could assist in resolving issues and improving project productivity. On large projects it is usually necessary to hold separate meetings with those most closely involved to discuss the issues in detail and manage potential risks.

When things go wrong:

Everything I have mentioned relating to project control is no more than simple arithmetic and common sense – so how can it all go so very wrong?

Our company was developing a computer system for a consortium of local authorities to enable them to collect the now infamous Poll Tax, otherwise known as the Community Charge. Our board of directors had been informed that the project was experiencing difficulties and they were anticipating a budget overspend of perhaps a few tens of thousands of pounds. I arrived at the project team office with a brief to determine the health of the project.

The room was a hive of activity, which is usually a good sign, but it was overcrowded and untidy (an outboard engine lay on the office floor). By the time I had completed my investigations it was obvious that the team had been at full stretch for some time – some members were already close to burn out – and there was still a lot of work to be done. Fresh thinking and fresh resources were obviously needed. This had been suggested before but the management had buried their heads in the sand and just hoped the team could pull it off.

There was very little budget left on a large fixed price contract and what was left was disappearing fast. I worked with members of the team to bottom out the problems and the work outstanding, and came up with a plan that required a significant injection of resources. We arrived at an estimate of over £1 million to complete the project. This bizarre situation had arisen because the work outstanding had not been properly estimated at regular intervals, and the management had refused to accept the reality that the project was way off track.

For my efforts in getting to the bottom of the situation, I was rewarded with the job of managing the remainder of the project. The pressure was intense, and trying to get all the local authorities to keep supporting our efforts and contribute more funding to the project was a major challenge. The financial aspects were handled by a board director with support from me, but I was able to focus primarily on delivering the system.

We did manage to deliver on time and some of the local authorities began to carry out massive processing runs to print out the next year's bills. At this point the Chancellor of the Exchequer stood up in the House of Commons and announced some last minute changes to the Community Charge – he was not our favourite politician.

We overcame that final hurdle and the bills were eventually all printed or re-printed by the local authorities in an acceptable timeframe. But that was not the end of the matter for me personally – a week later I found myself at the Old Bailey as a juror on a case involving the Poll Tax rioters in Trafalgar Square. I sympathised with their cause!

If a project falls behind schedule, or begins to cost significantly more than originally thought, the first reaction is often to send in the inspectors or the auditors. They will of course find some problems. The next step may be to replace the project manager, or perhaps to send in expensive consultants to resolve the problems. If significant financial losses are anticipated, the contract may be invoked and commercial and legal experts will then get involved. All of these possible scenarios will be a major distraction for the team attempting to maintain momentum on the project, and will result in a downward spiral of morale. In all likelihood the loss of morale will cause the project to fall even further behind schedule.

There are many reasons why a project may run into difficulty. If the underlying cause of this difficulty is a major imbalance in the triple constraint, no amount of inspecting, support or haggling will resolve the situation to anyone's satisfaction. The project will falter and may even come to a complete standstill. When this happens all momentum is lost, resources are redeployed elsewhere and much of the detailed knowledge about the project will have evaporated. It is very difficult and expensive to restart a project that has stalled.

A consistent drumbeat – estimating the work outstanding, measuring progress, preparing reports and holding formal meetings – is central to controlling the project. But there is another important element that needs careful management during the course of the project – *change*.

Change Control:

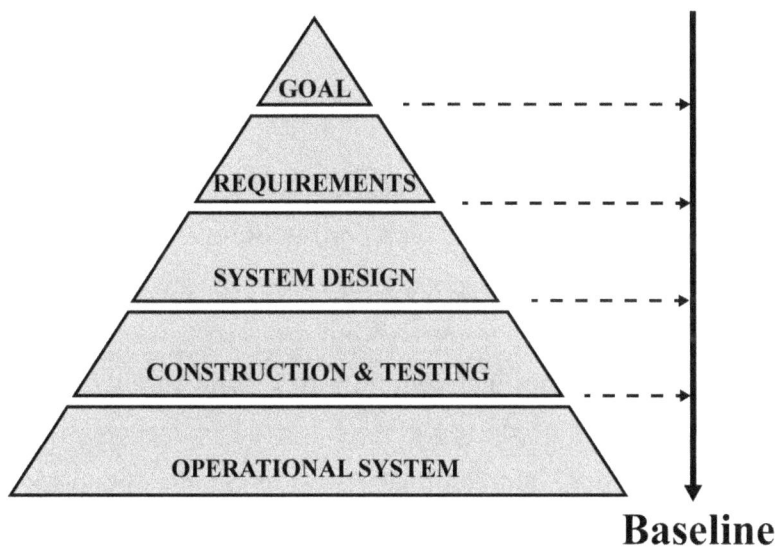

Baseline

The triangle above represents the emergence of detail as a project progresses through its life cycle; in this example – definition of the project goal, preparation of detailed requirements, system design, construction and testing, and finally an operational system. As the work progresses, more and more specifications, documentation and components are created and these will eventually define the final operational system. During the course of the project it is inevitable, except perhaps on very small projects, that some changes to the original requirements will be requested. Some of these changes may be critical while others may be "nice to have".

In order to control these changes we need to introduce the concept of a *baseline*. The first baseline is the definition of the project goal and its critical attributes. While changes at this high level are less likely than changes of detail, any that do occur could have a significant impact on the scope of the project. Changes relating to the critical attributes could have a major impact on design considerations, for example in the area of performance of the product.

The next baseline in this particular life cycle is the set of detailed requirements relating to the scope of the project. When initially produced, these requirements will have been approved and signed off by the appropriate authorities – but they may still be subject to change. The baseline then continues to expand throughout the remaining phases of the project until it is represented by the operational system – and this final baseline is essential for on-going maintenance and enhancement of the delivered system. Establishing and controlling an expanding baseline in order to manage change is fundamental in project work.

When a change is requested, it should be recorded in a *Change Register* in the first instance. Then an impact analysis needs to be carried out to ascertain the extent of the work that would be necessary if the change was to be implemented. If the project is still in the requirements phase, then the only impact will be to the requirement specifications. If it is in the design phase, the changes are likely to impact both the requirements and the design. As the project progresses, changes have the potential to impact many specifications and components that have already been created. If a change is implemented late in the project life cycle a considerable amount of rework may be required. For many projects it will be particularly important to carry out regression testing to ensure that the integrity of the overall system has not been compromised as a result of a late change. Regression testing is time-consuming and costly.

The *Baseline* is the foundation of Change Control and this concept needs to be clearly understood and accepted by those involved in the project, including all the stakeholders in the wider project environment. Many people who are unfamiliar with project work often have great difficulty in understanding why a seemingly simple change can result in a high cost of implementation. Educating them in the baseline concept and change control is the responsibility of the project manager, and this education should begin during the start-up activities and the earliest phases of the project.

When a change is analysed, consideration of the cost of making the change is obviously important. But equally important is the potential impact on resourcing levels, the critical path and the overall timescales. It is good practice, and essential on large projects, to allow for some level of change in the project costs and timescales when planning. Obviously it is not possible to be specific at the planning stage, but it would be naïve to ignore the possibility of change. It is common practice to include a specific fund for changes in the project budget that can be drawn down as changes are authorised.

On a large project a Change Committee should be formed and meet on a regular basis in order to prioritise and authorise specific changes. Approval should be given initially for an impact analysis to be undertaken since the work involved in the assessment of the change could be considerable. An allowance will need to be included in the change budget for the analysis of changes, irrespective of whether they are implemented or not. A change should only be approved when all the implications in terms of scope, cost and time have been assessed. Once approved, a change will need to be scheduled into the plans and then carefully monitored to ensure that it is properly incorporated into the finished product.

Change management can become very complex – it requires good processes and careful management. It is therefore important to plan for change and to budget for change. But even when robust processes are in place within the project, and contingency funds are available, the level of changes raised can become a major problem. If a large number of changes are required, these will clog up the on-going project work and severely impact its forward momentum. If this situation arises then the project is either not properly founded, or external factors are having a serious impact on the project objectives.

It is paradoxical that in a project that is creating rapid change, change itself should be a major threat to the success of the project

Project Management Life-Cycle:

Project management is often viewed as a linear function – planning, followed by executing the plan, and monitoring progress against the plan as the work progresses. In practice it is rarely that simple. Management of all except the smallest of projects is essentially cyclical, and the drumbeat is integral to that cycle.

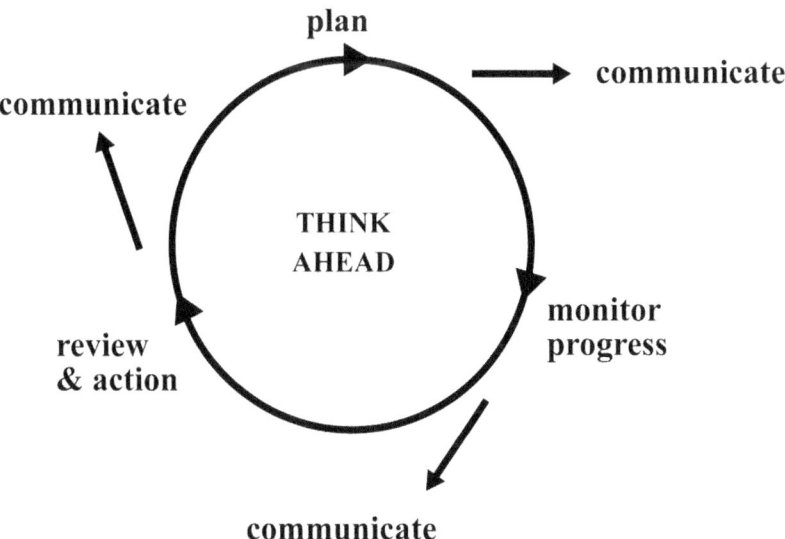

At the start of the project a detailed plan is developed and this initial plan is communicated to all interested parties. Progress against the plan is then monitored in relation to the original estimates and is communicated on a periodic basis as part of the drumbeat. Variations between the planned work and what is actually achieved will inevitably occur, whether through shortcomings in the work breakdown structure, the estimates, the level of resourcing or possibly the impact of change. The project manager continually reviews the status of the project and decides what actions need to be taken. The overall status of the project and corrective actions are also communicated.

If deviations from the schedule are significant, the plans may need to be adjusted. In the same way as the project documentation and components of the deliverables are base-lined in order to control change, it is common practice to baseline the plans. If reality drifts too far from the initial plans, continuing to measure progress against them becomes meaningless. In these circumstances the only option is to refresh the plans to reflect actual progress and outstanding work, and then to re-baseline the new plans and begin measuring progress from this revised baseline. Implications in respect of the triple constraint may be significant and will need to be clearly explained and understood by all concerned.

In addition to maintaining the drumbeat of the project management cycle, the project manager must continually look ahead to the coming weeks and months, checking that the material and human resources required to fulfil the requirements of the plan will be available as and when required. It is particularly important to think ahead before the project transitions from one phase to the next – at this time there may be significant changes to the organisational structure. There may be new resources to be inducted and absorbed into the on-going work of the project team, and/or existing team members to be deployed elsewhere.

The Human Factor:

So far in this chapter we have focussed on the processes that need to be adopted to control all the activities and tasks that are being carried out, and to communicate progress to the wider project organisation. This focus may give the impression of a production line of activities and tasks, and if this production line can be kept moving along we will eventually deliver the project. This is true to a large extent, but it is never that simple. We are dealing with real people in the project environment, not the resources labelled ano1, ano2, ano3 etc. that were identified when we drew up the original plans.

Real people have holidays, illnesses, training courses, babies, bereavements, divorces and any number of other events that are important in their lives. The diligent project manager will have incorporated as much into the plans as it is possible to know in advance – but unforeseeable situations will inevitably arise during the course of the project. One of the main problems associated with absences is the knock-on effect within the project team. Team members rely on each other in many different ways, for example to give instructions, to provide advice and support, to check work and to integrate the components that are being produced. It is after all a creative endeavour and collaboration between all team members is necessary to foster this creativity.

The project manager needs to be aware of impending planned absences and ensure that these do not unduly disrupt the work of others in the team. When unplanned absences occur, the project manager must assess the implications quickly and take whatever action is possible to reduce the impact. When the project manager is absent, a deputy should be appointed to keep the momentum going. These are all management actions that are necessary in all business environments, not just in projects. But the intensity of project work is such that the impact of absences is exacerbated, especially when important milestones are looming.

In all except the smallest of project teams there will be dissenters – those who are not prepared to put themselves out for the sake of project success. This is not a one week training exercise – a project may last for many months or even years. When everyone is working hard, late into the evenings and at weekends in order to achieve a milestone, stress levels will be high. Some people thrive on moderate stress while others find it difficult to cope, and the productivity across the team may become markedly uneven as a result. This may unsettle some team members and, although temporary, could result in underlying resentment.

The project manager must be alert to stress levels and to how individual members of the team are coping with the demands of the project. Failing to ease the burden when it becomes too great can have unfortunate consequences:

For the third night in a row I was hanging around the mainframe computer room in the City, waiting for the results of my latest test run. I had worked all day, but the project was at a critical stage and I needed to get the software bugs out of the programmes in order to meet the client's schedule. I expected to burn the midnight oil at this stage of a project – it was normal.

I was not alone that night. Another consultant programmer from my company was attempting to resolve the problems with her own programmes. She was working on a different project to me but was also up against a deadline. We chatted a little and she seemed quite calm, but as the night wore on I could see her pouring over the programme code for long periods.

I was eventually happy with my own test results and was preparing to go home, so I looked around to say goodbye. Her work lay on her desk, but she was nowhere to be seen. She had just got up and left and I never saw her again. She contacted our company a few weeks later to apologise, but she didn't return to work. The stress of late nights and looming deadlines had taken their toll – she had burned out.

It is not uncommon for a member of a project team to be unable to cope with the demands of the job. If this person is essential to the on-going work at the time, the project may be in trouble. If someone is burnt out and walks away, the chances are that a lot of knowledge and experience will walk away with him or her. Someone else will have to pick up the pieces and the effort associated with this will not be in the plans. Of course this type of problem can occur in any environment, but in project management terms it could mean the difference between meeting a milestone deadline or not. We must also remember that there may be serious consequences for the health of an individual team member who experiences burnout.

Problems may also emerge in the wider project context. Not everyone will necessarily be as enthusiastic as the project manager nor be prepared to make as big an effort to maintain progress according to the plan. When things are going well, most stakeholders will be reasonably co-operative when asked for extra effort at critical times. But if the project is running into difficulties, and there are rumblings on the grapevine, they may give a lukewarm response and wait to see how things develop. No-one wants to be associated with a failed project. This is not cynicism, it is realism. If the project organisation includes a project sponsor at a senior level, the project manager should invoke his or her support in adverse circumstances – sponsorship also comes with responsibilities.

Project Integrity:

It is not an offence to be behind schedule on a project. We know that reality will differ from our plans, that some tasks will exceed estimate, and that some aspects of the work will experience difficulty. Equally there may be other aspects that are going well and are likely to complete ahead of schedule – some tasks will require less effort than was originally estimated. The plans are the framework within which the individual activities and tasks are carried out, but the plans do not in themselves represent the integrity of the project.

It is always an offence not to know that the project is behind the planned schedule – if you are the project manager. If the planning has been carried out diligently, and control mechanisms to monitor progress are in place, then the status of every aspect of the work can be determined at regular intervals. There is no excuse for not knowing, to a reasonable degree of accuracy, how the project is progressing against the plans at every reporting period.

It is an even worse offence if the project manager knows that the project is behind schedule and decides to keep this information to him or herself. Nobody likes to give bad news, and some project managers may be tempted to avoid reporting slippage against the schedule on the basis that they think they can catch up later on. They just might get lucky!

The key point being made here is that project management is at the centre of the organisation established to control the project. The project manager should be fully aware of everything that is going on in his or her own dedicated team, and he or she should also be aware of events and activities in the wider project context. The project manager sets the tone for openness and integrity across the entire project organisation. A project team that embraces openness has a much better chance of overcoming the inevitable challenges than a team that operates on a "need to know" basis.

When a project is in difficulty, and a stressful situation has developed, the importance of good communications cannot be over-emphasised. If those who are associated with the project feel they are being kept in the dark, they may feel threatened and be reluctant to co-operate with the project management. However unwelcome the news relating to the project status, the project manager still has the responsibility to communicate this news honestly and accurately, and to communicate the remedial actions being taken. Many projects falter – that is a consequence of attempting rapid change – but many are subsequently repaired and eventually achieve the project goal.

The project manager holds the key to the project's integrity. No one else receives as much information relating to the overall project progress; no one else is in a better position to assess the implications of all this information; and no one else has the responsibility to communicate it effectively. If the project manager is seen to be open and honest, this attitude will permeate throughout the project organisation and encourage commitment and cohesion within the team.

**The Project Manager is the custodian
of the integrity of the Project**

11: End Game

We've made it!

There will be a lot of excitement and nervousness generated by the approaching climax to the project. The project team may have been working together for many months or years, and when the goal is finally achieved there will be a mixture of euphoria and relief. But before then it is essential that the project organisation is structured appropriately, and final plans are in place to cater for the countless details that must be attended to in order to get over the finish line.

Preparing the Ground:

Whatever the goal of the project, the product that is eventually delivered will have to fulfil a functional requirement of some description. The ground must be carefully prepared for the transition from development of the product to operational status.

If the product is a replacement computer system there will most probably be a data clean-up and a data conversion exercise to be carried out, training courses to be developed and delivered, and maintenance arrangements to be put in place for when the new system goes live. If the product is a new office building, the access routes, parking facilities, security arrangements, letting arrangements, cleaning etc. will all have to be available when the offices are opened. If a new vehicle is being launched, there will need to be trained mechanics in the field with access to spare parts, specialised tools, diagnostic equipment and maintenance manuals. Each project will have its own unique requirements and challenges in order to accomplish the transition from development to operational status.

The implications of introducing the product into the general environment should be considered in depth when the project goal is defined initially. Careful and detailed preparations need to be worked out in parallel with the project development work to ensure that the transition can be carried out safely and effectively. For large projects a separate "transition team" may be established to focus solely on these preparations; this team will have to keep abreast of developments on the project, for example the implications of changes.

It can be a major challenge to prepare for the transition from development to operational status, particularly in relation to timing. For example, creating a flight simulator for a new aircraft is a complex project in its own right. The simulator needs to be available to train the pilots long before the aircraft can be flown, but the final configuration of the simulator needs to reflect the completed aircraft. Another example relates to training courses for a new computer system. It is problematic to prepare training materials and deliver training courses without a fully completed product, but those who will operate the system need to be trained up in advance of delivery at a time when the system is still subject to change.

The Tipping Point:

Many projects seem to coast along without sufficient urgency in the early stages, in the mistaken belief that there is still plenty of time to catch up if a few delays occur. This is in fact quite dangerous and every effort should be made to get off to a good start. The start-up is usually quite challenging – for example the timely availability of the initial resources required by the plans may be difficult due to prior commitments. It is rarely possible to make up for lost time during any phase of a project unless some aspects of the original objectives are abandoned. Many projects will encounter difficulties during later phases of the life cycle, particularly during integration testing. The project manager may be forced to take some drastic action – either to extend the timescales or to reduce the scope & quality.

Re-planning and adjusting costs and timescales in order to accommodate unforeseen problems may be appropriate in many situations that develop during the course of a project, but this cannot continue indefinitely. Most projects will eventually reach some kind of tipping point, where success seems to be within reach based on the current plans. Eventually it becomes necessary to place a stake in the ground, focus on the approaching deadline, and go all out to get the job finished whatever it takes. This is the time to ramp up the efforts of everyone involved for the final push – and all projects will require this final push in order to finish off the work outstanding and to overcome the remaining hurdles.

Go/No Go Reviews:

In making the important decision to announce a firm date for transition of the product to operational status, it is essential to have confidence that the preparation work is sufficiently advanced, and that the product itself will be ready in time. The announcement of a date will inevitably trigger a number of other important activities outside the control of the project team – marketing initiatives and opening ceremonies being just two examples – and any delays at this stage could have very negative consequences.

It is therefore essential to approach this important decision in a controlled and reasoned manner. This can be done by setting up a series of go/no go reviews to monitor the remaining work on the product and the preparations being made for the transition to operational status. Anything and everything that could derail the live date must be considered as part of the go/no go review process. This process will normally be managed through a series of meetings that replace the formal progress meetings, but these will need to occur more frequently in the run up to live operation – perhaps even on a daily basis just prior to the deadline date.

For large projects it is a good idea to set aside a specific location, perhaps a room, for go/no go meetings. This can be used to display the last minute tasks and issues relating to product completion and also for transition – progress towards the deadline can be visually represented.

Live Operation:

Irrespective of how well the ground has been prepared, and the product tested, there is still one final and very large hurdle to overcome in order to achieve the transition to live operation. The nature of this hurdle will vary considerably depending on the type of project in question.

My own experience in IT is that there are inevitably very long and time critical processing runs to be carried out, and there is rarely sufficient computer power to achieve this comfortably. Quite often there is a major data conversion exercise to be processed and large databases to be populated. Other types of project will have their own specific constraints that provide major challenges at the final hour.

There are ways to reduce the extent of the breaking of new ground before live operation, for example:

Pilot scheme – transitioning to live operation is carried out for a small portion of the intended live theatre of operation.

Dress Rehearsal – emulating as much as possible of the live operation, but without the attendant business risks should things go wrong.

Parallel Running – operating a new system alongside an existing system that it will replace, and comparing the results to check that the differences are as expected.

Commissioning – operating at close to operational capacity in a controlled manner, for example test flights, sea trials and road tests.

Although the project is essentially "finished" by the time live operation is imminent, it is usually necessary to go back to the planning board one last time. What is required now is a micro-level plan for the cutover period to live operation, which may be just a weekend or a few days at most. This micro-plan will identify what needs to happen on an hour-by-hour basis, including a comprehensive checklist of tasks that need to be accomplished according to this timetable. It is prudent to incorporate a fall-back procedure in the event that things go badly wrong.

I always anticipate an exciting time towards the end of every project, especially at the point where we are running a new computer system in a live production environment for the very first time. This particular project did not disappoint:

Not for the first time I contemplated watching daybreak over West London from the 5th floor of our offices. It had been a

difficult two weeks finalising the system for a major client –
one of the largest employment agencies in the UK – and the
team had put in a big effort to get to this point. It was going
to be a long night, but our efforts would soon be rewarded
when we had completed the overnight production processing
successfully.

We had been having regular go/no go reviews over the past few
weeks, and only that afternoon I had agreed with the client's
finance director that we would run live that same night.
Processing would take all of the evening and several hours into
the morning, and the outputs had to be dispatched early next
day – there was very little contingency in the timetable.

All was going well with the evening processing runs, when one
of the software engineers informed me that he had discovered
a problem. This problem affected one of the programmes that
we would be running in the early hours of the morning. After
investigating the implications, it was apparent that this
problem was quite serious and had the potential to
contaminate a significant proportion of the production output.
We decided to try to fix it in time, and the software engineer
began work while I contemplated our options. None of these
options was palatable and the consequences of failure were
severe, for the client and for my own company.

I had worked with this software engineer many times in the
past and I trusted his judgement when he said that he had
fixed the problem. We ran some further tests together while the

clock ticked away. Making last minute changes to software is always risky, but I decided that we would put the revised programme into the production run – we had about an hour to spare.

I sent my colleague home – it would be too late to fix any other issues now – and I babysat the rest of the production run with a list of emergency phone numbers to hand. The production run went through successfully and the timetable was met. Not for the first time I watched daybreak over West London, and not for the last time had I made an important last minute call while playing the End Game.

Aftermath:

Irrespective of how well the project has been conceived, planned and executed, the end game will be a nail-biting time for all concerned. When the finish line has finally been crossed there may be a short period of euphoria, but it will probably be brief. The new product, now in an operational environment, will require careful bedding in and on-going support and maintenance – teething problems are inevitable. Those tasked with the operation, and those tasked with support and maintenance, should have already discussed in detail the processes required to fulfil their separate responsibilities, and the service levels to be achieved. But these support and maintenance processes will also need to be bedded in as part of the on-going operation, and support from the original project team members will be required in order to achieve this.

It is prudent to anticipate problems in the early days following the start of live operation, and it is unwise to let key team members go off on holiday or be reassigned. A help facility can be set up to ease the bedding in process, and a rapid feedback procedure is essential for major problems. A group of individuals with in-depth knowledge of the product, and with the necessary technical skills, should be on standby to act as a task force in the event of serious issues arising. It is good practice to have some of the project team present on site during the early days or weeks of live operation, to assist with familiarisation of the product and to liaise with the maintenance team.

The level of success achieved by the project will probably not be fully evidenced until some considerable time after the finish line has been crossed. Most organisations will aim to hold a lessons learned session after each project and may set up a repository of project experiences. This could prove of some use in the future, but not nearly as useful as the experience gained by those closely associated with the projects, and especially the project manager. Project work can be tough at times, but it is a good way to climb the learning curve very rapidly – for technicians, administrators and project managers alike.

Project success feeds our natural desires to take on even bigger challenges in the future – it's in our genes. We have already walked on the Moon, so it is only natural that our next goal should be to set foot upon Mars.

12: Critical Success Factors

Projects are challenging by their very nature, and there will always be many significant obstacles to overcome in all except the simplest of projects. The project manager must ensure that all the appropriate project management disciplines are employed in order to stay in control, but to some extent he or she will still have to "fly by the seat of their pants". There is usually so much happening on a daily basis when a project is in full swing and rapid decision-making is needed to keep the momentum going.

In this book I have tried to highlight the factors that are most significant in fostering project success – if we can't get at least these factors "right", we are unlikely to achieve success. The critical success factors discussed in the previous chapters are summarised below.

Project Goal:

The project goal must be clearly defined and understood by all stakeholders involved with the project. This requires the identification of the critical attributes associated with the project goal and their quantification wherever possible. It is through quantification of these critical attributes that the business case can be justified and targets set for the project team.

Stakeholders:

The individuals who have a stake in the project, for example those who will own and operate the end product of the project, those who pay for it, and those who must contribute to its success, all need to be engaged continuously throughout the duration of the project. Their input and support is vital to success in terms of meeting business requirements and performance criteria. Obtaining sufficient commitment from all stakeholders, and ensuring that the technical and business communities are working closely together, is one of the major challenges for the project manager.

Timescales & Costs:

After the project goal, timescales and costs are the highest profile aspects of all projects. Realism is important here. If timescales and costs are in the right ballpark from the outset, then the project has the foundations for achieving success – if they are over-optimistic the project will struggle to maintain credibility. Genuine effort put into work breakdown, estimating and planning will be rewarded eventually as the project unfolds.

Transition to Operational Status:

Whatever the facility, system or asset delivered by the project, there will be a potentially high risk event after which the end product will be required to support a business function of some description. The preparation and processes required to successfully get this business function up and running must be carefully defined and managed from the outset in order to ensure a successful transition to operational status.

Project Baseline:

In order to control costs and timescales it is essential to introduce the concept of a baseline into the project mindset – within the core project team and in the stakeholder community. The baseline starts with a clearly defined project goal, and then expands throughout the project's life cycle until a fully operational facility is achieved. Without this baseline it will be impossible to manage change effectively, with potentially dire consequences for the project.

Change Management:

A change management system must be introduced early in the project life cycle in order to control costs and timescales in relation to the baseline. The level of change needs to be monitored carefully. If it is too high the original project goal may become distorted, timescales and costs become untenable, and disruption to the ongoing project work become unsustainable. A Configuration Management System should also be introduced to control all the documentation and components created during the project, and to provide a sound platform for future support and maintenance.

Methodologies:

There is an increasing number of methodologies, techniques and tools to assist in the management of projects. Care is required to ensure that these aids are used sensibly and are not allowed to stifle the creativity that is a major ingredient of project success. Methodologies are a useful framework but are not a substitute for good management practices – they should be tailored to suit the project in hand, not followed slavishly. See Appendix III: Methodologies.

Risk Management:

There are several techniques and tools available for the analysis of risk and these can provide both quantitative and qualitative information. However their primary use is in documenting the risks and providing information for monitoring them. Real risks will not go away unless they are actively attacked by positive management actions, preferably before they mature.

Quality:

Quality is not an add-on to the project activities. It should be built into the fabric of the project from the outset and incorporated into the ethos of the project organisation. Everyone wants to be associated with success, but success will be elusive if quality measures are not implemented properly and quality is not apparent when the product attains operational status.

Team Building:

Thought needs to be given to creating a capable and efficient team with the right mix of abilities. Skilled resources required to satisfy the demands of project work are expensive and may not be readily available. Foresight is necessary to secure these resources as and when required by the plans. There are many recognised team building activities ranging from personality profiling to team celebrations at appropriate times during the project. Being able to obtain the right people with the right skills, and provide an environment that encourages teamwork, are probably the two most important factors influencing success.

Project Integrity:

All projects of significant size are high-risk undertakings and there are bound to be problems to overcome along the way. If there are no reported problems on a large project then communications are inadequate, and the project may be in serious difficulty. It is essential to create a positive attitude to raising and resolving issues throughout the wider project environment. The project manager must be aware of everything that is happening over the entire project organisation and communicate the status of the project clearly and honestly.

Project Manager:

Not everyone is suited to the role of project manager, and it is important to choose this individual carefully for the project in hand. He or she will need to understand the project from several different perspectives, not least from the business perspective. Experience will help greatly, but equally important is the energy and enthusiasm brought to the job by the project manager – he or she should feel comfortable in taking on the inevitable challenges.

13: Profile of a Project Manager

Virtual Project Managers:

Intelligence of Einstein – complex projects undoubtedly represent an intellectual challenge. The level of information that is generated, and that must be digested by the project manager, grows rapidly as the project progresses.

Patience of two saints – senior managers, stakeholders, suppliers, sub-contractors and core team members alike, all want information, support or attention from the project manager on a regular basis. This will try his or her patience almost daily.

Communication skills of Tom Peters – the project manager is the locus for all knowledge in relation to the project. He or she should be able to represent the project and its status from several different points of view, and to diverse recipients.

Planning skills of General Schwarzkopf – experience plays a large part in creating realistic plans for large and/or complex projects. Through experience it becomes easier to recognise what is achievable, and this is equally as important as detailed and elegant Gantt charts.

Charisma of John F. Kennedy – delivering bad news, seeking additional funding, convincing doubters that success is achievable, persuading reluctant team members to go the extra mile – these all fall under the remit of the project manager.

Skin of an armadillo – the project manager will never be universally popular. When work is ahead of the plans, some will say that the project manager has inflated the estimates to provide for an easy ride. When work falls behind schedule the project manager will be first in line for criticism.

Negotiating skills of a Mongolian horse trader – getting hold of the right skills and keeping them on the project may require some horse trading from time to time. When the going gets really tough it's time to take the gloves off and dig in the heels to get the resources that the project needs – some mild blackmail may even be necessary.

Real Project Managers:

The management of a large, complex, high value, multi-stakeholder, multi-disciplinary design and development project, comprising concurrent phases of activity and multiple sub-projects, and undertaken across geographically dispersed sites, will almost certainly place unrealistic demands on even a very experienced project manager. This description of the challenges facing project management is not untypical of many large projects undertaken in the modern world, and placing all responsibility for management on one individual is likely to result in loss of control.

In order to provide the right level of management for large and complex projects it is necessary to set up a project management team, with a Project Director heading it up, and several project managers reporting to this individual. These project managers may have particular knowledge and experience relating to the parts of the overall project for which they are responsible, for example Integration Testing. This project management team will need support from other specialised functions in their company such as Procurement, Quality and Finance.

The level of knowledge and experience required by a project manager depends primarily on the size and complexity of the project being undertaken. This has been recognised by the International Project Management Association **(IPMA)** and allied Associations in many countries throughout the world. The IPMA has established a 4 tier certification system that reflects different levels of competence in project management.

The Association publishes the International Competence Baseline (**ICB**) which currently describes a total of 46 different competencies that relate to the management of Projects, Programmes and Portfolios. These competencies are grouped as follows:

Technical:

There are 20 competencies in this group, examples being:

> ➢ Project requirements and objectives
> ➢ Control & reports
> ➢ Problem resolution
> ➢ Risk and opportunity
> ➢ Changes

Behavioural:

There are 15 competencies in this group, examples being:

> ➢ Leadership
> ➢ Openness
> ➢ Conflict & crisis

Contextual:

There are 11 competencies in this group, examples being:

> ➢ Business
> ➢ Personnel Management
> ➢ Law

Competence in this context is a combination of **knowledge** and **experience.**

The IPMA provides certification opportunities for project managers based on their competence in relation to the ICB. Certification levels A, B, C and D are offered, each successive level requiring a higher degree of competence in the required topics.

APM is the Association for Project Management based in the UK. The APM provides opportunities for similar levels of certification as the IPMA, based upon its Body of Knowledge **(BoK).** The Body of Knowledge describes the functions carried out during the management of Projects, Programmes and Portfolios – it currently covers a total of 69 topic areas.

Appendix I

Bid to Project

Two upwardly mobile managers from a large IT services organisation decided to go on a bear hunting trip in the Rocky Mountains. One was a successful sales manager and the other a project manager. On arrival at their chosen campsite – a small clearing in the woods – the sales manager suggested that he scout around for some bears, while the project manager sets up camp.

With the camp all set up the project manager waited for the return of his companion, and news about the bears. Suddenly he heard a crashing and roaring sound from the woods, getting ever louder. Presently the sales manager came running into the clearing with a large angry bear in hot pursuit. He ran straight past the project manager, calling out as he did so, "Here's the first bear – you skin this one and I'll go look for the next".

It sometimes feels just like that for a newly appointed project manager. While the bid manager and his team are out celebrating the success of signing up a large order, the project manager is combing through the bid proposal and contract, and trying to get to grips with the monstrous project that he or she must deliver.

Sales are of course the life-blood of all commercial organisations and a steady flow of new business is essential. The bid manager's responsibility is to win business that is profitable, but there may be exceptional cases where winning the bid takes precedence over making a profit from it. This could be the case when it is hoped that this particular piece of business will lead to future large orders, or perhaps open up a new market for the company. In many bid situations the level of information provided to potential suppliers is limited, perhaps sufficient to get an overall feel for the size of the job, but not enough to formulate detailed estimates and plans.

Large bids in particular are often managed using a sub-set of project management disciplines. The objective is to deliver the bid, covering a defined scope, within a limited timeframe. In an ideal situation there would be a seamless transition from bid to project, with the bid manager taking on the role of project manager for delivery once the business has been won. But in most organisations sales oriented individuals and project managers follow distinct career paths, and acquire different competences.

If circumstances allow, it is prudent to include the project manager designate in the bid team, at least for the later stages of the bid process. In some situations the customer will insist upon meeting the project-manager-designate as part of the bid process. Some customers may even insist on meeting several prospective candidates for the role and choosing one themselves – this is usually referred to as a beauty parade. If the project manager is involved closely with the bid then the quality of estimating and planning is likely to be enhanced. Similarly, if individuals with the technical skills relating to the proposed project are involved with the bid, and then move on to become part of the project team, a degree of valuable continuity is achieved.

When the business has been won, the transition to a project should be carried out in a controlled manner. The project manager needs to understand the basis upon which the business has been contracted and the commercial implications of the triple constraint – there may be penalties for late delivery of some or all of the scope. So there is a lot of reading to be done, and meetings to be held with the bid manager and members of the bid team. It is good practice to arrange a formal *start-up meeting* as part of the transition, where members of the bid team and key members of the project team get together to exchange knowledge and ideas.

There will be a lot of information for the project manager to absorb and a multitude of things to manage when the project is started up. There will be many people to meet – members of the customer's organisation, suppliers, stakeholders from the wider project environment and prospective team members. The project manager needs to keep a cool head at this crucial time and think through the project from start to finish at a high level. There may be a prescribed methodology mandated for the project – methodologies are discussed in Appendix III – but in their absence reflection based on the various chapters in this book will be useful. There will be a pressing need to begin employing project management disciplines in a detailed way and to get the work started, but it is also important that the project manager keeps the big picture in mind from the outset.

Not all projects result from a bid process. Company internal projects may arise from feasibility studies initiated by senior managers and executives. There may not be any specific commercial constraints associated with these projects, for example contracts with penalties for late delivery. But this can be a disadvantage – commercial imperatives provide a strong incentive for everyone involved with the project to achieve success. Irrespective of commercial considerations, all of the project management principles described in this book will apply to internal projects. Expectations in terms of scope, cost and timescale are often set during the formative phase of a project, and at some point a project manager will be assigned to deliver according to these expectations. A controlled start up process is equally important for internal projects.

Appendix II

Project Life Cycles

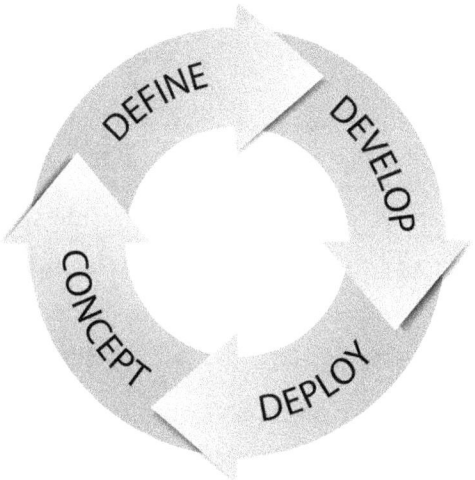

Projects evolve through a natural progression from high level concept, through detailed evaluation, design, and creation of specific components. These components are then integrated and tested before the final product is transitioned to an operational environment. To facilitate control of this progression projects are divided into phases or stages, each phase having its own specific objectives that must be achieved before moving on to the next phase. There are several recognised life cycles that are frequently applied within particular industries, but there can be no hard and fast rules – every project situation is different and will require careful consideration before deciding upon the most appropriate life cycle. A non-specific life cycle is represented as follows:

> ➤ Concept or Feasibility
>> ➤ Definition of Requirements & Outline Design
>>> ➤ Detailed Planning
>>>> ➤ Design & Build
>>>>> ➤ Testing & Integration
>>>>>> ➤ Handover & Close out

Concept or Feasibility:

This phase is carried out to study the business context of the proposed project and to evaluate the business implications should it be undertaken. A list of high level requirements will be produced together with some broad estimates of the likely timescales and costs, and possibly a high level plan. At this stage the detailed work to be carried out is largely unknown, and timescales and costs will be based on similar projects completed in the past, or on not much more than guesswork. The main deliverable from this initial stage will be a Business Case or Feasibility Report, which should include a statement of the Project Goal and its Critical Attributes.

Definition of Requirements & Outline Design:

During this next phase the implications of carrying out the project are investigated in more detail and a set of detailed requirements is developed. These requirements will cover the functional and technical aspects of the proposed product and also requirements relating to its operational status. During this phase an outline design is developed together with a high level plan for the next phases of the project.

If the intention is to put the project out to tender, an *Invitation to Tender* document is prepared to enable potential suppliers to present their bids. The responses to the invitation to tender are normally required in a prescribed format to facilitate comparison with responses from all potential suppliers by the client company. These responses may include quite detailed plans developed by the bidding suppliers – the level of detail in the plans reflecting the information provided in the invitation to tender document – supplemented with the supplier's previous experience in this field. Firm estimates of timescales and costs are normally mandated by the client company. A period of negotiation with one or more of the bidding companies will follow before a contract is awarded to one supplier.

Detailed Planning:

Although expectations in terms of timescales and costs may already have been set in previous phases, it is during this phase that the triple constraint can be more confidently modeled. The life cycle for the remainder of the project is determined, product and work breakdown structures are developed, activities and tasks estimated, dependencies identified, resource requirements analysed and a schedule produced. All costs associated with the project are calculated. The Project Organisation is created and roles and responsibilities defined. Control mechanisms such as progress reporting, change control and financial control are decided.

Design & Build:

This is the phase when project resources are ramped up quite rapidly to undertake the design and build work. Design of the product or deliverable will be carried out in detail and the individual components specified and developed. Depending on the nature of the product the design may be completed in detail before build work commences, or some proto-typing and overlapping of design and build may be appropriate. Training materials and operational procedures are drafted.

Testing & Integration:

The components that comprise the product created during the previous phase are assembled in a suitable test environment. They are tested together as a whole to ensure that the product meets the original requirements and also meets the design objectives and constraints. This is a crucial phase and will expose any weaknesses in the original design and in the build quality. In addition to testing the integrity of the product as a whole, it is essential to test it together with other entities that will impact upon it in the operational environment for which it is destined. Training material and operational procedures are finalised during this phase.

This phase of the project often comprises two elements – initial testing of the integrated product by the project team, followed by acceptance testing with the participation of the customer.

Handover & Closeout:

The transition to live operation is accomplished and the ongoing support and maintenance commenced. Imperfections, bugs, snags – anything that has been identified as a shortfall during testing and integration – are listed, and responsibilities for correction are negotiated with the customer. A schedule for the rectification of these issues is drawn up and agreed.

The above life cycle is of necessity quite generalised – in practice the life cycle will be tailored to the job in hand. Phasing the project in this manner provides for checkpoints along the way and aids control of the overall scope, timescales and costs. But phases naturally overlap during the course of a project. It is important to view the project as a continuum of endeavor and to prepare the ground for each phase well in advance of it actually starting in earnest.

Appendix III

Methodologies

Methodologies are often mandated for all projects carried out in large companies, especially if these companies are providing project based services to clients as their primary business. The best known project management methodology at the present time is PRINCE 2 and there are several training courses available to explain how this can be applied in practice.

However, many large businesses have developed their own methodology, specifically designed to suit the type of project that they are engaged in on a regular basis. When fully developed, these home grown methodologies will extend their influence beyond the immediate project environments into the financial, commercial and quality functions of the business.

Methodologies have a number of advantages, but potentially some unwelcome side effects:

Advantages:

A methodology provides a framework that ensures projects are carried out on a consistent basis and that the same processes, techniques and tools are used throughout the company. It also ensures that documentation is created for the same purpose, and in the same format, across all projects. This consistency of method makes it easier for stakeholders and senior managers to understand project management terminology and the progress information provided to them.

The project manager does not have to create processes for every new project – for example change control, quality control, risk management – and familiarity with the mandated tools increases productivity. The format of progress reports and the reporting of financial information can be standardised. It is therefore easier to transfer management and team members between projects as they will already have some experience of the processes, techniques and tools in use.

Methodologies enable centralised control within the business for all project based activities. If it is decided to make a change, for example to the financial reporting requirements for projects, this can be initiated centrally by updating the methodology. The change can then be promulgated throughout the company by re-issuing all or part of the methodology. Training courses based on the methodology can be designed and delivered to project managers, stakeholders and project team members as a component of employee development.

Side Effects:

If not sensibly developed and implemented, methodologies can end up burying the project team in paper or the electronic equivalent. This may be accompanied by a high level of administrative overheads and bureaucratic dictates.

Methodologies can give the illusion of control, where in fact no real control exists. The necessary checklists may have been completed, the mandated specifications, reports and quality documents prepared, all according to the prescribed processes – but this does not guarantee the appropriateness and accuracy of the information contained within them. Following the methods precisely may give confidence that the project is carrying out its work according to the rules, but this does not mean that the project team is working efficiently or that the final product will be fit for purpose.

Project teams are sociological entities and creativity is an essential ingredient for achieving a successful outcome. If members of the project team are focused primarily on the bureaucratic imperatives of a methodology, there is a distinct danger that this essential creativity will be stifled.

Summary:

Methodologies are unlikely to be a perfect fit for every project undertaken by a business. They need to be sufficiently comprehensive and prescriptive in order to achieve a good level of control over projects, but not so onerous or inflexible that they suppress the sociological and creative ingredients necessary for success.

Appendix IV

Earned Value Management

Earned Value Management (EVM) is a control process that establishes a baseline for performance measurement initially, and facilitates reporting of a project's status in terms of scope, time and cost as the work progresses.

Baseline Costs:

The scheduled cost of the project is shown as an *S-Curve* – a visual representation of expenditure over time. Work and associated costs normally take time to build momentum during the early stage of a project and then slow again as the project nears completion.

BCWS: Budgeted Cost of Work Scheduled – The Baseline

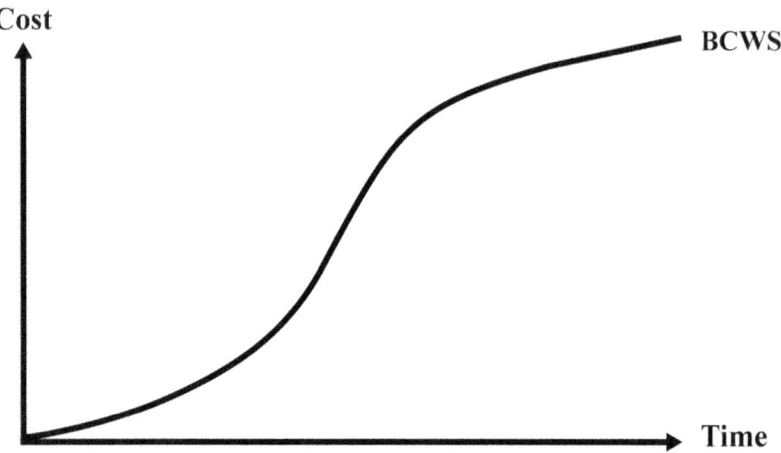

The graph above illustrates the cumulative work and associated cost over the course of the project, as predicted in the plans prepared at the start. This is the baseline against which progress is measured.

Cost Variances:

The following refer to cumulative costs up to a particular Reporting Period:

> **BCWP:** Budgeted Cost of Work Performed
> (or EV = Earned Value)
> **ACWP:** Actual Cost of Work Performed

The following refer to the status of the project at a particular Reporting Period:

EAC: Estimate at Completion
CV: Cost Variance
CVP: Cost Variance %

The following example illustrates how these values can show trends across several reporting periods for a project with an initial budget of 300:

RP	BCWP	ACWP	CV	CVP	EAC(1)	EAC(2)
1	10	10	0	0%	300	300
2	25	35	−10	−40%	420	310
3	40	60	−20	−50%	450	320
4	100	120	−20	−20%	360	320
5	180	230	−50	−28%	383	350
6	260	320	−60	−23%	369	360

The Cost Variance (CV) = BCWP – ACWP and shows overspend or underspend on the work done to date.

The Cost Variance % (CVP) = the Cost Variance as a percentage of the Budgeted Cost of the work done to date (BCWP)

The Estimate at Completion EAC(1) = the ratio of the actual spend to the budgeted spend (ACWP/BCWP) for the work done to date, multiplied by the original budget. This calculation is based on the assumption that the over or under expenditure to date continues at the current rate for the remainder of the project.

The Estimate at Completion EAC(2) = the original budget adjusted by the Cost Variance (CV) to date. This calculation is based on the assumption that the remaining work is performed at baseline cost, i.e. no further overspend or underspend occurs.

EAC(1) can be considered as the pessimistic (or realistic) view, while EAC (2) can be seen as the optimistic view.

The values for CVP show that the project was exceeding budget at an ever increasing rate up to period 3. Overspend was contained **in relative terms** over the next three periods.

Schedule Variances:

The following refer to the status of the project in relation to the time schedule at a particular Reporting Period:

SV: Schedule Variance
SVP: Schedule Variance %

RP	BCWS	BCWP	SV	SVP
1	10	10	0	0%
2	20	25	5	25%
3	50	40	-10	-20%
4	100	100	0	0%
5	200	180	-20	-10%
6	280	260	-20	-7%

The Schedule Variance (SV) = BCWP – BCWS and shows whether the work actually performed up to the reporting period is greater or less than the work originally scheduled, expressed in terms of budgeted costs.

The Schedule Variance % (SVP) = the Schedule Variance as a percentage of the work scheduled to this point (BCWS).

The values for SVP show that the project was on or ahead of schedule up to period 2; fell behind schedule in period 3; was back on schedule in period 4; and then fell behind again.

The Cost and Schedule variances can be represented in graphical form to provide a visual comparison with the original baseline cost. The following two graphs are not related to the tables above.

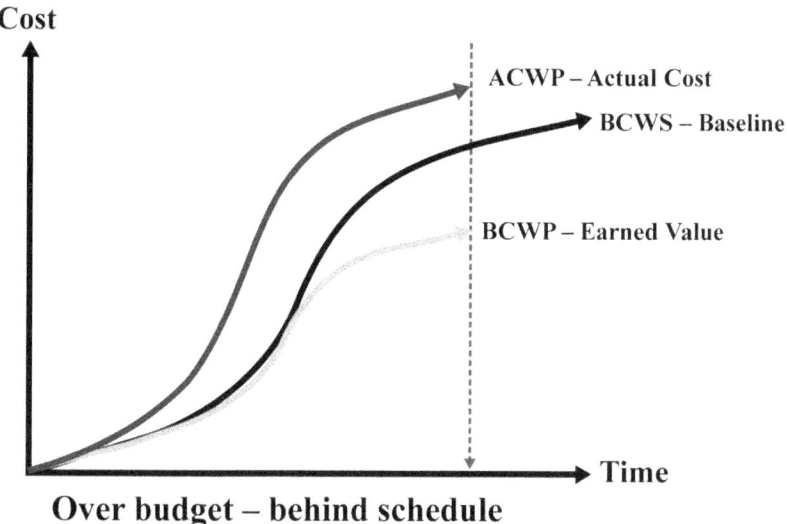

Over budget – behind schedule

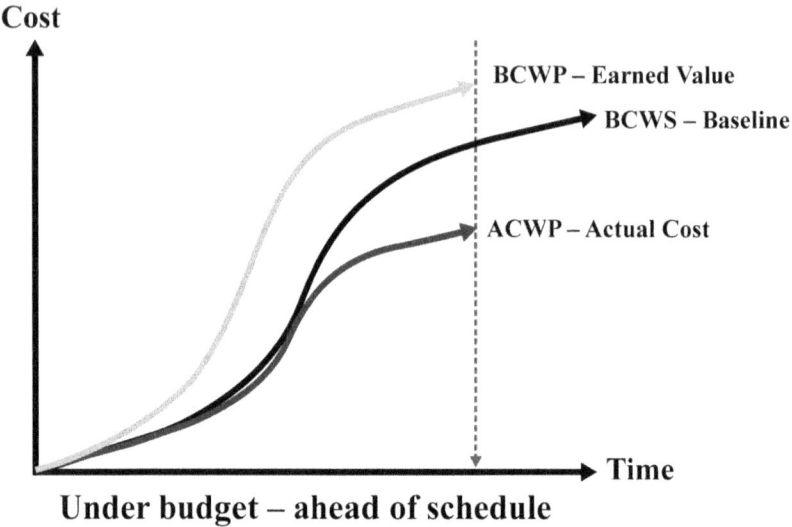

Under budget – ahead of schedule

A graph that shows BCWP and ACWP following the Baseline precisely indicates a project that remains exactly on budget and on schedule every reporting period – a highly unlikely situation!

Performance Indices:

CPI: Cost Performance Index

SPI: Schedule Performance Index

CSI: Cost-Schedule Index

RP	BCWS	BCWP	ACWP	CPI	SPI	CSI
1	10	10	10	1.0	1.0	1.0
2	20	25	35	0.71	1.25	0.89
3	50	40	60	0.67	0.8	0.54
4	100	100	120	0.83	1.0	0.83
5	200	180	230	0.78	0.9	0.7
6	280	260	320	0.81	0.93	0.75

The Cost Performance Index (CPI) = BCWP/ACWP. An index of 1.0 indicates on budget; less than 1 indicates over budget; greater than 1.0 indicates under budget.

The Schedule Performance Index (SPI) = BCWP/BCWS. An index of 1.0 indicates on schedule; less than 1.0 indicates behind schedule; greater than 1.0 indicates ahead of schedule.

The Cost-Schedule Index (CSI) = CPI x SPI. An index of less than 1.0 indicates that the project is experiencing difficulties.

The CPI and the SPI represent the variances in a slightly different way from the cost and schedule variances illustrated previously.

In the table above:

> - in period 2 the project is over budget and ahead of schedule
> - in period 3 the project is (more) over budget and now behind schedule
> - in period 4 the project is (less) over budget and on schedule

The interpretation of the values calculated by the Earned Value method is equally as important as the values themselves. For example:

> - a project that is over budget but ahead of schedule may be acceptable if the timescale is critical

> ➤ a project that is under budget but behind schedule may be acceptable if the timescale is not critical
> ➤ a project that is significantly over budget and significantly behind schedule requires remedial actions.

About the Author

Jim Mackay was born in Dunfermline, Scotland shortly after the end of the Second World War. He studied Mathematical Sciences, Earth Sciences and Psychology at the University of Edinburgh before moving to England to begin his career.

After a few years working in the Meteorological Office, he embarked on what was to become a long and successful career in Information Technology. Having initially gained technical expertise in the design and development of information systems, he moved on to develop competency in the management of projects.

Over the course of a 40 year career he has managed many large IT projects in a variety of business sectors including Finance, Insurance, Energy, Human Resources, Distribution, Central Government and Local Government. He has been instrumental in developing a project management methodology, has developed and delivered training courses and presented on many aspects of project management. He is an independent consultant and an assessor for the IPMA's (International Project Management Association) certification program.

His knowledge of project management disciplines and extensive hands-on experience of managing complex projects has provided him with the vital insights illustrated in this book. These insights are enhanced by descriptions of real life scenarios that he has encountered during the course of his career, and which highlight his pragmatic approach to projects and their management.

Jim met his wife Cica while they were both working in Libya. They subsequently moved back to the UK and made their home in London. They have been married for over 30 years and have two daughters – Vesna and Daniela – and two grandchildren.

www.ingramcontent.com/pod-product-compliance
Lightning Source LLC
Chambersburg PA
CBHW051503170526
45166CB00001B/370